THE CST WAY

John Marcarian
Founder
CST Tax Advisors

The CST Way
By John Marcarian
BEc, CA, M Int. Tax (Hons), ACIS Dip C.M.

Head Office
CST Tax Advisors Pte Limited
Level 17
96 Robinson Road
Singapore 068899

The CST Way is brought to you by
CST Tax Advisors

Asia • Europe • US

www.csttax.com

PRAISE FOR THE CST WAY

As the CEO of a digital marketing agency – my personal experience with CST Tax Advisors has been of great service and professionalism. This book really captures how CST Tax Advisors works for us. The CST Way is 100% what you look forward to in a professional services firm. The stories are terrific and the approach John articulates will make you wish CST Tax Advisors was part of your team.

Ash Aryal
CEO & Co Founder, Quantumlinx

The CST Way for me is also about leadership. I know John and his team have been showing a passion for tax since I have known them. The book is a clear and concise treatment about how to run a professional service business. A terrific tale of client service.

Greg Chappell,
Former Australian Cricket Captain, Australian Test Selector

I have experienced The CST Way for over a decade now. I think the book captures the care, empathy and focus that CST Tax Advisors brings to the market. I commend you to read the book if you have an interest in customer service and business studies.

Mark Cullen
Head of Internal Audit, Deutsche Bank

The CST Way is exactly how John and the team have looked after me for nearly a decade. Passion, empathy and

accountability is 100% what the CST Team show on a daily basis. A great read.
Michael 'Mile' Jedinak,
Captain of the Socceroos, Australian National Football Team

I have been a big fan of The CST Way for more than a decade now. The book is a great read and John captures perfectly the way that the global team delivers on its commitments to clients and the broader community.
Rod Lappin
Senior Vice President – Lenovo, Asia Pacific

Having known John the Founder of the CST Tax Team for over 15 years I can say that The CST Way is a terrific story about a dynamic group of professionals. This is how they do it. This is how they live and work. It's a great book and a must read for people who like stories about business and service delivery.
Sidney Minassian
Contexti

I have known John for more than a decade and he runs a terrific global company. As my accountants CST Tax Advisors has made a major difference to my financial and tax management. This book The CST Way is a wonderful expression of how they do it. I love the stories and anecdotes. The material is innovative and that sums up the guys at CST very well.
Michael Rebelo
Chairman and CEO, Saatchi and Saatchi Australia

I was first introduced to the CST Tax team in London in the mid 2000's. Since that time I have come to admire their global business. Not only do they deliver a great service to clients around the world but also their unique operating methodology means international solutions are seamlessly delivered. I have worked with them in Asia and Europe and I believe The CST Way tells it as it is.
Allan Reeves
Celerity Group

Everything's changing and disrupting today. Globalisation can't be reversed. So no matter how savvy you think you are, you'll find yourself in one of the stories in this very readable book. You'll probably then break out into a cold sweat. But at least you'll have the remedy in your hands.
Diane Smith-Gander
Director, Wesfarmers Limited

Since I have worked with John and his team I have come to appreciate The CST Way as truly unique in how they do things. Accounting firms typically don't take such a wide-ranging approach to global expat and international tax. The CST team is different and this book is a testament to their uniqueness. Definitely worth a read.
Travis Smithson
CEO, Argonaut Securities Asia Limited

ABOUT THE AUTHOR

By his mid-teens, John Marcarian read his first book on international tax planning and was hooked. John has since become a chartered accountant, international tax adviser and the founder of the global business CST Tax Advisors.

Throughout his youth, John developed a keen interest in business, sport and travel. At the age of 27, John founded what is now CST Tax Advisors.

In 2004, John established the first international office of the company in Singapore. Since that time, CST Tax Advisors has spread to many global locations. The company remains the only business that focuses solely on the tax needs of global expats living throughout 'Expatland'.

A regular speaker, John travels internationally, presenting numerous technical and business papers to organisations such as the American Australian Association, AustCham Singapore, Israel-Asia Chamber of Commerce and Australian Business (in London) to name a few.

John has worked with private clients in more than 50 countries to date.

In 2015, John launched his first book, Expatland, as a guide for those planning to move to live, work, or study away from their home country.

In 2016, John founded CST's own charity, 'Expatland Giving Back', which works with expats, their friends, and families to help give back to their local communities.

For further information, visit www.expatlandgiving. org

John is married, with two daughters. In his spare time he is learning Brazilian, Portuguese, and how to surf.

.

DEDICATION

This book is dedicated to the many people who have helped me build my vision of The CST Way into a reality.

I have been blessed to work with and for some immensely talented people at my previous professional firms. My early mentors, Peter Allsop and Richard Elkan at Duesburys, inspired me to build a career in professional practice. Joe Bongiorno and his brother, Tony, taught me many things and I learned commercial lessons working with them that I carry with me always.

It has been a pleasure to work with all of my people at CST Tax Advisors (from Vicky Hoffman, 1993 and onwards). Nothing develops one's leadership skills quite like leading others on a journey, and at the end of the day, that is what The CST Way is all about – a magnificent journey.

My gratitude and deep appreciation go to my brother, Matthew, who left a promising career at KPMG to join me at CST Tax Advisors in the year 2000. Matthew has tremendous technical and commercial ability. Apart from being my right-hand man, working with him is a joy. I am also extremely fortunate to have met my other brother-in-arms, Peter Harper, in 2010. Peter is very talented, not only in international tax, but also in business building and overcoming challenges. His courage and commitment, as we work together globally, is an essential part of our success.

To all our principals at CST Tax Advisors, I thank you for helping me build this remarkable company. Special thanks to my friends, Boon Tan, Geraldine Chapman, and Feroze Sukh. They are people I can always count on for help and support.

Most importantly, my thanks go to my lovely wife, Taleen, and my wonderful daughters, Isabelle and Natalie, whose support has been without limitation while I traverse the hills and valleys of Expatland. They are the motivation for all that I do.

To Mum & Dad

With love and thanks for showing me

The Marcarian Way

AUTHOR'S NOTE

For the sake of protecting privacy, most with a couple of exceptions, the names mentioned in this book have been changed. The stories and their locations, though, are generally just as they happened.

FOREWORD

When John asked me to write the foreword for *The CST Way*, it came as a pleasant surprise that there was an international tax company at which someone had read my book *Traction* and implemented EOS (The Entrepreneurial Operating System), the system I created.

The surprise was due to my experience that most accounting firms don't generally make the best candidates for implementing EOS because of the way they're typically structured.

After discussing CST with John, I learned that his global leadership team has a strong commitment, focus, and passion for *Traction* and EOS. They believe that this is one of the reasons that they're doing so well globally.

Before speaking with John, I hadn't heard about the country called "Expatland." It was interesting to hear that it's the fifth largest country in the world, with over 244 million residents.

Without question, people moving around Expatland expanding their businesses need a solution such as *The CST Way*.

Expatland is a concept that resonates with me because so many entrepreneurs move away from their home countries to expand abroad. Without a doubt, these people need specialized guidance and support in the area of tax accounting and finances.

John's vision of Expatland is innovative and unique. His first book, *Expatland*, is all about planning for the move to Expatland and how to succeed when you get there. For over 25 years, John has been building a business that brings unique focus and service offerings to a global client base.

The CST Way is a great read for any entrepreneur who is moving to Expatland, as well as any potential partner firm or future employee looking to work with John's dynamic global accounting firm.

Gino Wickman
Author of *Traction* and
Creator of EOS

SPECIAL INTRODUCTION

As the CEO of one the major global trust and corporate services firms, and the only one with its HQ in the heart of Asia it is my pleasure to write this special introduction for John's second book, *The CST Way*. Being a client of CST Tax Advisors makes it personal for me also.

While I live in Hong Kong, I do spend a lot of my time, traversing the globe to visit the many markets in which we operate or to encourage new people and firms to join our fast growing firm.

In our professional life, the 2,500 employees in my firm work closely with financial intermediaries and, in particular, with international tax advisers.

So we have seen the full spectrum of tax advisers - those operating in one market, those operating across many countries, those operating under a "one firm" principle, and those who share the same name but in reality are really a loose confederation of franchise operations around the world.

We know a thing or two about what makes a good tax adviser and the quality of advice and service they offer.

As this book bears out, in a practical, easy-to-read style, CST fits very much in the category of a global firm with a common vision, a true consistency of approach wherever clients work with them, and a deep commitment to build long-term relationships with the many individual and corporate clients operating in Expatland.

Expatland is the term that John has coined to describe perfectly the place that those people with global aspirations (and the guts to follow their dreams) wherever that takes them live.

What's great about *The CST Way* is that it accurately describes the way CST works with its clients.

John and his team should be commended for building a firm that reflects 100% the philosophy he has to doing business. That's why his firm continues to grow and yet stays true to the values as set out in this excellent book.

Martin Crawford
Group CEO
Vistra

TABLE OF CONTENTS

PREFACE

BEGINING OF THE CST WAY

"Whenever God wants to give us a gift, he wraps it up in a problem.' – Dr Norman Vincent Peale

At 27 years of age, I was stoked. I had just agreed to terms with Deloitte Touche Tohmatsu to join their Sydney Tax Practice from Westpac Banking Corporation where I was a Tax Manager. It was early 1991, I just got married, and was full of hope that a great career with a Big 4 firm was on its way.

How wrong I was.

At the time, I had neither heard of nor understood the wisdom of the above quote.

Within three months of joining Deloitte, the tax partner who had sought me out from Westpac delivered me some feedback that led to me founding my firm.

His feedback was that helping corporations' executives with their own personal needs was not Deloitte's focus. Deloitte's client was the corporation, not the executive.

My interest, though, was in helping the executive *and* the corporation.

To hear this message was disappointing.

Ever since I was a 19-year-old accountant within the Business Services Division at Arthur Young, I knew that building strong client relationships was a key part of service delivery.

Helping the person in the corporation with their own needs seemed relevant to me in building a relationship.

At Arthur Young, we were private client focused. I remember going to visit clients, at their homes, with partners and managers. Often, we would sit around the proverbial dining table getting to the heart of what their family's financial and tax issues were.

This personal style of doing business continued at Duesburys, Chartered Accountants, where I worked for very personable and professional tax partners. Duesburys was a firm built from the gradual aggregation of smaller accounting firms. Therefore, they had the private client focus in their DNA.

In any event, my way was not the Deloitte way and I founded my firm Marcarian & Co (the precursor to CST Tax Advisors) on 1 April 1992.

God, indeed, must have wanted to give me a gift.

When I started out, the first part of the 'gift' was that my good friend, Theo, a finance director of one of my clients at Deloitte, followed me as a personal client of my new firm. Not only that, but Theo also brought all the tax work for his corporate employers.

These companies were United States (US) subsidiaries in the dental supply business. So, from the early days I had international clients.

Theo remained a good friend and a client until his retirement.

The undeniable truth of business development in a personal service business is that your success lies in how well you can form a personal, but professional relationship with the person facing you.

Early on, I focused on individual and private client tax and accounting services for clients living in Australia. I soon realised, however, that many of my friends living and working overseas with Australian and non-Australian assets were looking for a personal tax and advisory service that covered not only Australian tax, but also international tax.

Many of my clients were now being sent to work in London, Hong Kong, Singapore and Japan.

While I had initially focused on their Australian tax and accounting needs, I started noticing that they shared many common objectives, regardless of where they lived and worked around the world.

My clients were looking for someone who would be able to help them – not only from a compliance perspective, but also with broader international tax compliance and planning issues.

For example, they needed my help regarding which structures would best hold their assets, and advice about how their income and assets would be taxed in their home market (Australia) and in the country where they worked.

One client provided me with an early insight as to where my future lay.

His name was Hanu Korhonen.

Hanu was a Finnish resident with investments in Australia, Singapore and London. One of my first tax plans was to advise Hanu's Australian subsidiary in relation to its dealings with its Finnish parent company.

I must admit that I had doubts about how I would be able to help Hanu given I had no experience in Finnish tax.

I remember finding and speaking to a Finnish accounting firm over several late nights to identify the key tax issues that needed to be planned for, and which issues would impact on Hanu's business in Australia.

I recall being surprised by the contrast between the Finnish and Australian tax systems. The concepts were so different.

I was struck by the power of one idea. It was this: when it came to examining two international tax systems, it was vital for an advisor to be able to work collaboratively with a foreign tax professional to understand and integrate ideas and the laws of both jurisdictions to help the client.

Integration was essential.

With Hanu as a client, I came to appreciate the challenges facing not only business people setting up in Australia, but also expats and other Australian business professionals establishing themselves overseas.

The early 1990s was a time of great tax reform in Australia. It was a great time to be building a tax business.

Australia had just brought in major pieces of new tax legislation, including the Foreign Investment Fund regime, the Controlled Foreign Corporation regime, and the Transferor Trust rules.

The complexity of these new laws meant that Australians investing internationally for the first time needed to pay much more attention to how they implemented their business plan and how their international tax strategy would evolve in line with this.

I spent the next 12 years building the business in Australia (before expanding CST Tax Advisors overseas in 2004), and our team worked on many aspects of the accounting profession, including international tax, accounting, tax advisory, trust and company formation.

From the outset, our core focus was to help private clients and family business owners expand at home and abroad using an integrated 'two-country' advisory model.

Built into our firm's DNA was the need to go the 'extra mile' for our clients and to think about questions that we would want answers to if the roles were reversed and we were the client.

My intention is that as you begin Chapter 1, *'Philosophy of The CST Way'*, you will develop an appreciation of our business approach and how it works in action.

I am grateful to Hanu, my first overseas client, for sending me on the journey that has become *The CST Way*.

CHAPTER 1

PHILOSOPHY OF THE CST WAY

''We have a passion for tax, we engage
with empathy, we are accountable for our
performance.' – John Marcarian, Matthew
Marcarian, Peter Harper

*The phone rang at 5pm on 22nd June 1998 to deliver
the news I was waiting for. The Board of Directors of
a listed major Australian film production company had
just signed the guarantee I had pushed for. We had a win.
Now to tell my client the good news.*

The backstory to the above was that one of my major clients, Henry Kennedy, a CEO of a European Bank based in Australia, was investing in a film project with a major Australian film production company.

A partnership was being put together for the various investors to join. The partnership was taking on certain external liabilities and obligations.

The basis of the project also included the obtaining of a tax deduction for investors in the film partnership. On the surface, it was an attractive proposition.

However, based on the documents I reviewed, I saw some major flaws.

One of the major flaws was that nowhere in the documents was there a guarantee (by the listed Australian film company) that if the partnership's business (which they were managing) did not work and liabilities exceeded assets, that my client would not be pursued personally.

Both our client's financial advisor and his lawyer missed this point.

Henry was also keen to 'get a deal done' by the looming 30 June deadline so that he could claim the income tax deduction in the tax year.

Henry thought he would be okay as he was dealing with a public company. I was not, however, happy with his commercial exposure.

To make matters a bit more challenging, Henry was about to leave for a golfing holiday at St Andrews in Scotland – so getting the transaction documents to him was going to be fun. However, accountability for performance and a passion for tax demanded that I could not 'green light' the investment, unless I was comfortable with the tax and legal risk.

I briefed outside legal counsel to draft a formal guarantee for the public company to sign.

Needless to say, this caused great consternation at the investor group level.

A single accountant for one investor was holding up a group of 20 investors (domestic and international) in a major film project that needed to be signed off before 30 June 1998.

Welcome to my world!

I received some concerned phone calls from Henry (pre-tee off at St Andrew's golf course) and a few more calls from other legal and tax advisers for the other clients who thought we were delaying.

Henry, however, was investing well over A$1m (quite a bit at the time). I knew that, with the circumstances, they could not proceed without his funds. I held my line on pushing for the provision of the guarantee.

In the end, the public company blinked and they signed the guarantee signed on Friday 25 June 1988. That was great news, but now we had to get the documents signed by Henry.

My challenge was then to spend most of Friday night (morning time in the United Kingdom (UK)) getting a notary from Edinburgh to drive to the Royal and Ancient Golf Club at St Andrew's, and locate Henry on the golf course. I believe the notary found Henry as he was about to tee off on the famous 'road hole', the 17th hole of the course.

Thankfully Henry signed the relevant documents just in time.

Needless to say, this was accountability and passion at the coalface. My passion for tax, Henry's passion for golf!

The place where we deliver The CST Way is in Expatland.

Let's take a tour.

Expatland: Where we live

Expatland is the name I have given to the special 'country' where global expats live and grow their businesses. It is a 'country' with more than 240 million people of different nationalities from all over the world.

If it were a single country, it would be the fifth largest in the world after China, India, the US and Indonesia.

Here are just a few interesting facts about Expatland:

- Almost 6.5m US expats live abroad, while 38m expats live in the US.

- There are now more than 4.5m Britons living and working abroad.

- Some 41 countries each have a British expat population of 10,000, while 112 countries have at least 1000. Many of these are working in non-English speaking countries, such as the Gulf States, China, India, Brazil and other emerging economies.

- Eighty-five per cent of more than one million expats in China work for international firms, with the largest proportions in sales and marketing (30 per cent), banking (25 per cent) and engineering (15 per cent).

- In the past two years alone, the number of Spanish expats in Brazil has doubled, and increasingly Britons are following suit with the UK being the fourth largest investor in Brazil.

- By 2025, 70 per cent of the global workforce will be people born after the year 2000.

- The 'millennials' are particularly attracted to the UK (19 per cent) and the UAE (16 per cent) as locations to live and work.

- The VITM (Vietnam, Indonesia, Turkey and Mexico) countries are presenting expats with exciting prospects for career progression.

- More than 53 per cent of expats agree that VITM countries are improving rapidly as places to live and work, which is perhaps indicative of the more attractive relocation packages offered to these employees.

- Out of the four VITM countries, expats in Indonesia (31 per cent) are most likely to be on secondment – more than three times the global average of 7 per cent.

We understand that Expatland is full of global citizens who are travelling to establish businesses or work or study more widely than at any other time in history.

The need for cross-border taxation, accounting and structuring services for global expats and international enterprises is significant and growing.

Who do we help?

We help globally-minded individuals and businesses owners who leave their home country to live, work or establish business overseas.

We understand this broad class of person needs international tax, accounting, and structuring services.

Examples of our clients include:

- a senior corporate executive pursuing an employment career in Expatland

- a business person moving to establish a foreign business in Expatland

- an investor seeking to live in Expatland for lifestyle and/or family reasons

- a professional pursuing broader international experience

- an academic teaching or on a course of study

- a franchisor setting up an overseas business network

- a businessperson relocating their business from their home country.

All these people require international tax advisory, accounting, business advisory compliance and structuring services at some stage.

Key Questions asked *The CST Way*

In implementing *The CST Way*, a useful starting point is to consider two key questions:

1.   *R-Factor Question®*

2.   *What Can Go Wrong Question*

1. The R-Factor Question®

The concept of the *R-Factor Question®* was developed by Dan Sullivan and is a registered trademark of The Strategic Coach Inc. Dan has shown how answering this question is a most effective way for professionals to help people progress in all areas of their lives and their businesses. For more details on the *R-Factor Question®*, please visit: http://blog.strategiccoach.com/dan-sullivans-r-factor-question/

From my perspective, this question is all about assisting you to form a relationship with a friend, client or co-worker.

Asked at the right time, the *R-Factor Question*® is a powerful question that helps us identify areas our client may need our help with. It provides us with an insight into their personal or family objectives.

The *R-Factor Question*®is:

If we were meeting three years from today – and you were to look back over those three years to today – what has to have happened during that period, both personally and professionally, for you to feel happy (satisfied, content, pleased, fulfilled) about your progress?'

The R stands for relationship!

As our philosophy is working with empathy, we develop a strong relationship with our clients. The R-Factor Question® is a good way to begin.

The power of this seemingly simple question stems from its open-ended nature.

We believe that if our clients answer this properly, it will reveal a lot about their objectives.
It requires them to have the perspective of someone 'looking back down the valley' that they (our client) have already walked through.

As such, they are visualising what has already happened and are sharing it with us.

Our aim here is to guide our client to come to the question with thoughts about what has already happened.

For example, in answering this question, a business client might say:

A) I have established a branch of my business in London.

B) I have bought an investment property on the Upper East Side in New York.

C) I have employed a general manager to run my Hong Kong business.

D) I have completed my Masters in Finance.

E) My family and I have taken a vacation to Mount Kilimanjaro.

F) I have developed a tax strategy to support my business in the US.

The question provides very clear information about how our client sees progress and where we can help.

Our job as tax advisers and accountants is to identify the client's objectives we can help with and those which we cannot.

One of Dan Sullivan's great messages is to *'focus on progress, not perfection'*.

This is a very useful reminder for our clients. They will not meet all their goals overnight. It is a process.

I highly recommend working with Dan Sullivan's materials for anyone keen on building very strong relationships with clients. I have had the privilege of working with Dan's great materials for many years.

Today our management team uses a wonderful system devised by Gino Wickman known as the Entrepreneurial Operating System (EOS). The EOS is explained exceptionally well in his awesome book, *Traction®*.

Whether you are a business owner, a not for profit, or just seeking to get more out of your life, Gino's book is a terrific read. At CST Tax Advisors, we enjoy working with his material.

We are often asked to ensure that other professionals 'come to the table' and help our clients with services beyond our remit, whether they are insurance professionals, private bankers, lawyers or migration agents. We are there to help clients achieve their objectives. Client's answers to the *R-Factor Question*® give us signposts to show us the way to help them

It should be clear then that we are never on the 'opposite side' of the table to our clients in terms of our approach. Rather, we take a 'same side of the table' attitude, as we are both looking forward to achieving their personal and business objectives.

We deliver our services with the following objectives in mind:

- Creativity
- Flexibility
- Responsibility
- Leadership

i)   Creativity and flexibility

The services we provide are creative, flexible and practical.

Solutions for clients sometimes need to be created outside of the traditional method or the typical way of doing things.

Our approach is to provide a wider range of options – heightening flexibility for our client.

Often a client needs a foreign holding company established to buy a foreign business. We generally conduct a review of three to five jurisdictions to determine the best outcome for our client. We will work with complementary service providers as and when necessary.

Clients respond well to solutions that give them 'optionality'. Unsurprisingly, they also respond well to solutions that show thought and consideration for their personal circumstances.

We are passionate about tax.

ii) Responsibility and leadership

When we work with our clients, we take responsibility where appropriate. We believe we should take a position rather than present a range of options and let our client decide.

By expressing a view and providing reasons for that view, our client can then assess whether to accept our leadership on the relevant tax, accounting or business strategy solution.

We do not believe that shying away from leadership is consistent with our Guiding Philosophy. Showing leadership is often what clients are looking for in the process of making financial decisions.

We are accountable for our performance.

The What Can Go Wrong Question

Since the early days of my practice, I took the view that when advising a client, if you take them through all the things that can go wrong and address these fully as a professional, then our client's 'downside' has been covered.

The approach of covering a client's downside when looking at a broad international tax and business planning exercise is essential.

Not considering the bigger picture and not asking the *What Can Go Wrong Question?* can leave clients exposed in several areas.

The *R-Factor Question*® does not give rise to our client thinking about the *What Can Go Wrong Question?*. Separate work needs to be done on the worst-case scenario for a client.

In my experience, if you have covered the downside, then the upside is all there is left to focus on.

To further illustrate the point with the *What Can Go Wrong Question?*, let me discuss a case of a new client that came to see me in Singapore in the early days of our business.

Our client wished to expand his business from Singapore to Hong Kong.

For the sake of the story, the business plan called for the manufacture of 'widgets' in Hong Kong and their supply into China and South East Asia. At our initial meeting our client said, 'I just need tax advice from CST Tax Advisors about expanding from Singapore to Hong Kong'.

Our client presented me with an impeccable business plan; it was beautiful to look at and it read well. Nevertheless, when I asked our client the *What Can Go Wrong Question?*, our client was bemused and he replied, *'Nothing can go wrong – I have done months of market analysis. I have my distribution agreements in China and Asia lined up; my key staff and I know my manufacturing costs. All good.'*

Undeterred, I asked our client the following questions:

Question 1: Do you have a co-shareholder in the Singaporean company?
A: Yes – there are three of us.

Question 2: Do you have a shareholders' agreement?
A: No – we are all school friends.

(This is a major weakness. The absence of a shareholder agreement means in the event of dispute in terms of the way the

41

business is carried on, there are no clear rules about how disputes might be settled.)

Question 3: At present, who are the signatories on the bank account for the company?

A: All three directors must sign cheques.

Question 4: Have you given anyone a power of attorney or enduring power of attorney so that in the event of your mental incapacity that person can act for you?

A: No.

(This is a major issue, because the company bank account would be inoperable if my client loses mental capacity, but does not die. Note that an enduring power of attorney provides that a person may make decisions on behalf of another person when they have lost mental capacity.)

Question 5: Do you have Hong Kong-based directors?

A: No. We will run it from Singapore.

(Not having any directors in Hong Kong and running it from Singapore means that the Hong Kong company is taxable in Singapore – a point my client had overlooked).

Hence, just by asking five questions, I demonstrated quickly that our client was unprepared in several key areas. There were serious weaknesses and exposures that this client had not considered.

This shows how important the *What Can Go Wrong Question?* is.

Merely confining ourselves to what our client came to see us about is not *The CST Way*. Our client had real exposures and these had to be pointed out and dealt with.

This takes empathy.

The question can be asked repeatedly in many areas, business and personal, to understand which risks must be covered as part of assisting clients to manage their tax, accounting and business affairs.

The *R-Factor Question*® gives us pointers about how to assist, but the *What Can Go Wrong Question?* hones in on all the remaining and urgent areas for professional attention.

Some of these areas will involve us as tax advisers, but more often than not, other professionals will need to be drafted in to work on solutions for our client.

43

The powerful effect of considering everything that can go wrong for a client – doing our best to cover it and then working on our client's *R-Factor Question*® responses – means that we are well placed to deliver on our *Guiding Philosophy* mentioned above.

.

Doing it *The CST Way*

- We have a passion for tax – we engage clients with empathy – we are accountable for our performance.

- We use the *R-Factor Question*® – we need to understand the journey you are on.

- We ask the *What Can Go Wrong Question?* – we cover the downside.

- We base our advice on our clients completing the Fact Finder – a key data collection document used by our professionals working with clients.

- We design creative and flexible solutions for our clients.

- We take responsibility and we show leadership in our recommendations.

CHAPTER 2

EMPATHY, UNDERSTANDING AND COFFEE

'When you show deep empathy towards others, their defensive energy goes down, and positive energy replaces it. That's when you can get more creative in solving problems.'
– Stephen Covey

The smell of black coffee permeated the house as my friend Mary sat next to me. She watched her brother, Michael, recount how his business was collapsing so rapidly that soon he would be bankrupt and he would have to sell his wonderful family home. His marriage, his business and his settled family life were about to come to an end.

In that moment, I understood the simple truth that although, at times, we are completely powerless to affect an outcome, empathy is the bedrock for a successful client relationship.

Unfortunately, Michael did go bankrupt.

Michael was not a client of ours he would never have been in that position if he was), but as Mary was our client, I did what I could to help.

I went with Michael to see many of his former business associates. We spent many hours trying to work out a rescue plan for him with banks and law firms.

What I saw over those few months was the unseemly side of how the absence of empathy can fail to rescue not only a business, but also a person's good standing in his community.

People that stood next to Michael in the good times exhibited a complete and wholesale lack of empathy when he hit trouble. Now they ran the other way.

Mary's relationship with CST Tax Advisors spanned more than 15 years. As a result, our relationship grew stronger due to the many hours I put in trying to help her brother and the empathy that we as a business showed Mary's family,.

Sometimes, it is not what you do that matters – it is how you do it that matters.

'Empathy, understanding and coffee' is an unusual chapter title, but it explains our approach to our relationships with clients – namely collaborative, personal, and warm.

Empathy in our approach is essential.

Empathy is the bedrock of all our client relationships. It starts with how we engage clients at the beginning of our relationship. It is part of the everyday client experience.

From our first meeting and by asking the R-Factor Question® and What Can Go Wrong Question?, we demonstrate this.

One of our key skills is our ability to work and think 'outside the box' across many markets in order to give our client the best possible solution for their circumstances.

We cannot solve individual needs for clients without adapting and changing our advice for their unique circumstances. There is no such thing as a standard solution to a situation.

In line with our philosophy, our obligation is to ensure that if we cannot provide a particular service to our client, then we are frank, open and honest about it.

Furthermore, being able to communicate 'bad news' well is essential in maintaining a good relationship. It sounds strange, but it is true. Anyone can deliver good news.

A person's success in maintaining relationships is often dependent upon how well they can deliver bad news. If we have bad news to convey, then we are always empathetic in how we deliver that news.

We always consider how we ourselves might like to receive it.

Bad news should never be delayed, shelved or covered up. Doing so does not engender trust.

The importance of having a regular cup of coffee (or tea or mineral water!) to build empathy and understanding is crucial.

Main aspects of our client experience

Many clients come to us for help and guidance in situations that can affect their finances. Often, they do not know exactly what help they require or what questions to ask.

Therefore, we consider their complete financial situation, enabling us to fully assess how we can provide assistance and ensure we can empathise with their situation.

The Financial Questions

As noted above, part of our early process is working through the *R-Factor Question®* and the *What Can Go Wrong Question?*

After we have worked through these questions with our client, we also take time to discuss and understand their balance sheet and income position. Generally, this information has been provided to us in advance of the initial meeting.

During this initial meeting, asking open questions helps us *and* helps our client understand their short-, medium- and long-terms goals, which we will collectively work towards achieving.

What Information Do We Need?

For personal tax work, we always ask clients to complete our Fact Finder document, which contains numerous questions relating to assets, liabilities, dependants, date of birth, insurance, superannuation and current professional advisers (legal and financial).

Importantly, the Fact Finder provides a place where clients record their objectives and reasons why they are coming to see us.

We do not begin an assignment without having a completed and signed Fact Finder document in our possession. We may also delay taking on a client until we have had an initial 'whiteboard session'. The whiteboard session is our term for the initial meeting we have with a client (usually because there is an electronic whiteboard in our meeting room!).

I have learnt that advising on incomplete information is fraught with risk and the likelihood that some issue will be missed rises substantially.

Over the years, I have found that the initial whiteboard session is essential in building trust. Everything is up there, on the board, for all to see – assets, liabilities, income, objectives, and plans for action.

I am a great believer in having the spouse or partner in attendance. Having a couple in the office always brings out more issues than either one singularly.

Importance of Our Client Experience

Many of us have been on the wrong side of poor professional treatment. We know when we are left feeling 'processed' and given 'standard advice' or 'cardboard cut-out solutions'.

Without all the information gathered in the Fact Finder, we cannot effectively perform to the high standard we deliver to our clients.
The initial experience a client has with us establishes the basis for the long-term relationship.

A good first meeting allows us to obtain information on a more personalised basis and to give advice on all financial decisions that will be entrusted to us.

As so many new clients come to CST Tax Advisors at the recommendation of our current clients, we value the responsibility of on-boarding new clients properly.

In some cases, we need to show leadership and assist our client to take control of building their tax, financial and business agendas. Our experience can often help our client determine what needs to be done and *when* it needs to be done. This is because our expertise in international tax, accounting and structuring issues enables us to highlight serious technical risks or opportunities ahead of our client.

Should our client suggest that they wish to undertake actions that we do not agree with for tax or other reasons, it is our obligation to discuss these concerns with our client and positively influence their behaviour as best we can.

If our client still wishes to continue with actions or undertakings in relation to a tax position we do not agree with and which is incorrect, we are regrettably obliged to resign from the engagement.

Given the risks of carrying on business in today's world, we cannot continue to act for a client who does not respect our views and advice. This is particularly the case when it comes to tax.

Doing it *The CST Way*

- Empathy in our approach is essential. It is the foundation stone of our client relationships.

- Our obligation is to ensure that if we cannot provide a particular service to our client, then we are frank, open and honest about it.

- If we have bad news to convey, we deliver it faster than good news.

- We do not commence an advisory assignment without a completed Fact Finder.

- Our initial whiteboard session is essential in building trust.

- Given the risks associated with global tax advisory, we do not act for clients who do not respect our views and advice or who do not provide answers to all the questions we ask.

CHAPTER 3

HOW WE CAN HELP

'As you grow older, you will discover that you have two hands: one for helping yourself, the other for helping others.' – Audrey Hepburn

'We need your firm's help moving our business to Europe, Asia and the US', Tony said in a matter of fact way as he looked out across the water from the Fullerton Bay Hotel in Singapore.

The night before, Tony had told me he was flying into town for meetings with the Asian heads of global internet companies. He asked if I could see him straight after his meetings.

Although we had some general knowledge about business models that derived internet search revenues, we were soon wrestling with the complexity of understanding how the 'source of income' rules varied in different countries.

We spent much of the next three months working, as a global tax team should, on the global solution for Tony and his fellow stockholders. It was clear the business was expanding rapidly and that the advertising and search revenue opportunities for the business required a global tax firm with skills in multiple markets.

While I worked to establish the Hong Kong licensing company and other trust structures for certain revenue streams, my brother Matthew formed the head office company in Singapore while considering treasury and other objectives. Peter Harper, our US business head, and I worked closely on the US-Australia-Asia flow of funds.

Tony and his team were already doing business. We did not have time to lose. They could not wait.

We quickly put in place a basic structure that could be modified as we worked through the group's objectives.

The work was intense and it needed to be done in rapid time.

It involved us coordinating the work of lawyers and accountants in various locations where we were not based, including Uruguay and Venezuela.

Tony and his team were very appreciative that we could execute on the tax compliance, tax advisory and accounting work that was required in their five markets.

We held meetings with Tony and his executive team in multiple locations – San Francisco, New York, Sydney, Singapore, and Hong Kong.

Over the ensuing months (and given our passion for tax), we were true to our central goal of 'making life easier abroad'.

As a team, we combined very well and delivered in our niche area, which is integrating global tax and accounting solutions.

The CST Way is to begin by focusing on the big picture and working down.

Focus

Focus means that commencing from 40,000 feet, we can see the 'big picture' in a client matter, then after implementing discussions regarding the *R-Factor Question*® and the *What Can Go Wrong Question?*, we can work our way down to a more granular level.

The importance of focus cannot be overstated. All client situations are unique; focusing and thinking about an individual client's facts are essential parts of *The CST Way*.

Focus requires an in-depth knowledge of our client's position.

Focus is the foundation of proper tax and business planning.

If a client's wealth position is not commensurate with their age and business status, this should trigger some concerns at our end. It may be that our client is looking for our help in setting up an introduction to a wealth advisor and/or is in need of help in relation to budgeting or managing cash flow. We are in an excellent position to introduce our client to qualified financial planners, private banks and other specialists who can help with our client's progress.

<u>Initial Tax Review</u>

A good way of looking at the 'big picture' is via an *Initial Tax Review*. This gives us an opportunity to engage with a client and do a high-level overview.

The Initial Tax Review would provide written guidance and strategies on how our client might proceed, based on the issues brought up in the initial meeting.

This is a general document that will deal only with what was discussed in the initial meeting. It does not provide detailed analysis and planning for the issues covered.

Importance of the Big Picture: Why We Do It

Focusing on the big picture helps us identify ownership and location of assets and what tax-planning issues will arise. For example, a family home in Australia with a large mortgage is inherently tax inefficient, because the interest is not tax deductible.

Focusing on the big picture gives us the opportunity to determine what assets can be restructured, whether debt or equity can be repaid, or whether debt can be refinanced or refocused for the benefit of our client.

One of the primary goals of delivering a professional service to a client is to reduce our client's exposure to legislative risk while helping them achieve their objectives. There is an inherent advantage in managing tax risk that CST Tax Advisors brings to Expatland.

We understand both international and domestic tax laws and how these can assist our client. This is the CST difference.

How we do it: the Strategic Tax Review

Once we have understood the 'big picture' and undertaken an *Initial Tax Review*, the next step is a *Strategic Tax Review*.

This is a process in which we identify areas and issues relevant to our client that they need to focus on from our perspective. We then outline solutions and options.

The *Strategic Tax Review* is a comprehensive documentation of all issues relevant to our client, the legislation that impacts them, and possible solutions and implications.

We do, in specific cases, bypass the *Initial Tax Review* for a client if their situation requires immediate in-depth analysis.

The *Strategic Tax Review* addresses our client's taxation and legislative position and considers their specific objectives outlined in the Fact Finder, their responses to the *R-Factor Question®* and the *What Can Go Wrong Question?*.

.

Doing it *The CST Way*

- The importance of focus cannot be overstated.

- Focus requires an in-depth knowledge of our client's position.

- Focus is the foundation stone of proper tax and business planning.

- A good way of looking at the 'big picture' is through our Initial Tax Review process.

- Focusing on the big picture helps us identify ownership and location of assets and high-level tax-planning issues that will arise.

- One of the primary goals of delivering professional services is to reduce our client's tax exposure to legislative risk, while helping them achieve their objectives.

- We understand both international and domestic tax laws, and how these can assist our client.

- The Strategic Tax Review is a comprehensive document of all issues relevant to our client.

CHAPTER 4

THE PRIVATE CLIENT: THE WHO, THE HOW, THE WHY

'Great artists need great clients.' – I. M. Pei

As I pulled into driveway of the Ferraro brothers' building in Parramatta, Western Sydney, on 10 July 2005, I was sure there would soon be fireworks. My clients were two Italian brothers who had worked together peacefully for over 15 years. They were upstairs with separate lawyers about to argue over the breakup of their company.

I knew the who.

The Who

Mario and Gino were second generation Australians from Sicily. Their parents, Frank and Appollonia, migrated to Australia in the 1950s. The brothers built a large building products business together after leaving school. Mario started first and Gino joined him.

They imported and distributed building products throughout Australian and Europe. It was a big business.

In Sicilian culture, the older brother is generally respected and listened to and that cultural bond had worked to hold things together until today.

Both brothers had their spouses working in the business. They also had a sister, Mary, working in the business. Mary was head of corporate sales.

How had it come to this I wondered?

The How

Over the last 12 months, since Mario established a subsidiary company in Italy, I knew the brothers had stopped talking to each other. The weekly phone calls between them had ceased.

The monthly phone calls between the brothers and CST Tax Advisors had ceased. Growth in Australia had slowed, because Mario was travelling to and from Italy more often, and he was focused on the European business. This created more tension, because Gino was left to carry the burden of the Australian business.

This failure to communicate eventually manifested itself in the brothers calling me to pass on important messages to each other, even though they were equal shareholders in the same parent company.

After 2 years, Gino had enough of the losses Mario was making in the Italian operation – so he wanted to either sell his holding or buy Mario out and close the European business.

He asked me to call a meeting at their headquarters and ensure that Mario and his family were present.

I arranged the meeting for December when Mario and his family traditionally visited Sydney to see the rest of the family.

The 'how it came to this' was seemingly a result of business losses and a failure to communicate.

Now it was time for me to understand the why.

The Why

I entered the boardroom of the company head
office in Sydney and it was like a scene out of The
Godfather.

Around a long rectangular oak table sat both families.
Mario, his wife Janet, their family lawyer, and adult
children were on one side of the table.

Gino, his wife Tracey, their adult children, and their
family lawyer were on the other side of the table.

Tellingly, though, their sister Mary sat with Gino.

Gino opened with his first salvo. Gino made it
known that he believed Mario had been stealing
from the company for almost two years, and that
he only opened the business in Milan to cover the
fact that he was using company stock to build his
new holiday home on the Amalfi Coast.

Wow!

This was a great way to start the meeting. Things
descended from there.

Mario told Gino he had been carrying him for 15
years and that Gino did not deserve all he had
earned from the company. I watched while this
back and forth went on understanding that 'the

why' was indeed very much more complicated than it initially appeared.

What began as a concern about a 'trading loss' soon became a long and involved story about holidays, unpaid leave entitlements, sabbaticals, and many issues over the previous decade.

At the end of the meeting, it was clear that Gino had documentary evidence of Mario's 'borrowing' of stock through the European operations. Such borrowing was not documented and Gino believed this was intentional.

The 'moral right' was with Gino.

It was decided that Mario would sell his shares to Gino and leave the company for two reasons:

- Firstly, Mary – older than both brothers – chastised Mario for this 'borrowing'. She would not work with Mario.

- Secondly, Gino and Mary had the support of their mother who was still alive and unknown to me. She was, in essence, a silent 'chairperson' from a distance. When I understood the why, the course of action was just, equitable, and plain for all to see.

While our clients, generally, have service expectations that relate to income tax planning and compliance and/or accounting assistance it is the who, the how and the why that tells the real story of private clients. Without understanding a client's family or business situation and the many factors in their lives – professional service delivery risks becoming mechanical, distant and not client centric.

We always respect the who, the how and the why.

Let me now discuss some specific areas to consider when dealing with individual private clients.

Processing an individual tax return

When working on our client tax returns, we ensure that we do not waste time dealing with irrelevant information, data, or incomplete forms.

We make sure that we have all the necessary financial records. Where there are transactions that we are not clear about, we dig deeper.

Understanding our client's personal circumstances means that we know if something that has been classified as a 'work expense' may actually be a 'private expense', and hence not tax deductible.

On many occasions, we advise clients that certain expenses are tax deductible. This news is always well received!

We understand that clients are not tax advisers and they rely on us.

If there is doubt in relation to the veracity of a claim, we do not claim it.

An individual client (much like a company or trust), has an income statement and a balance sheet. We make it our business to know their financial position. We never commence our client's individual's tax return unless we have reviewed our client's Fact Finder documents.

In terms of a new client engagement, we examine tax returns for our client for the past three years before starting to prepare the current income tax return.

This gives us a sense of key background information in relation to our client's financial affairs.

We think for our clients. In the case where a new client is 'on-boarded' at CST Tax Advisors, we examine their records prepared by the previous accountant to see what issues may lurk within their tax records.

In other words, proceeding to do compliance work without a complete understanding of the processes we are required to undertake is **not** *The CST Way*.

Tax Planning: What We Think About and Why?

Given that our clients live in Expatland, it is not unusual that assets are located in a number of different countries. Thus, they often have to do tax returns in other jurisdictions.

Often, we help our clients estimate their annual tax liability on a global basis by working with our international CST tax partner firms. Sometimes we assist our clients with managing their personal cash flows in order to meet their tax payment obligations.

We work collaboratively with related professionals who are part of our client service team.

In cases where CST Tax Advisors acts for our client in one country but not in another, we have a collegiate and respectful relationship with the other tax advisory firm.

In undertaking tax planning for our clients moving abroad, we recognise that we are often asked to identify and consider what opportunities exist for them to restructure their affairs.

In meeting this objective, we never put in place artificial, contrived or unrealistic steps to achieve a tax outcome.

When considering whether a particular structure or strategy is viable, we carefully examine the costs associated with the establishment of the structure, ongoing compliance costs, and any tax payable in relation to the transfer of the assets.

Having empathy with our client means that we also consider our clients' need to access capital if some unforeseen eventuality arises.

Life happens and having our clients' capital locked up in some structure, that cannot be of benefit or use to them, is not showing empathy.

Our general view is that a restructure of a client's asset holding position should only proceed where there is a tangible non-tax benefit resulting from the implementation.

Our approach is collaborative and we believe that regular contact with our client is vital.

Therefore, we hold regular meetings with our clients to update their Fact Finder documents and review the *R-Factor Question*® and *What Can Go Wrong Question?*.

Client Profiles

Global expats and international businesses form the vast majority of our client base. As such, our clients often consider acquiring assets either in their home country or in overseas markets.

We work with them to advise and implement an effective tax strategy that works from the perspective of their 'arrival' jurisdiction and their 'home country' jurisdiction.

Determining Tax Residency: Black, White or Grey?

While some residency cases fall into straightforward black or white decisions, often they slide into a grey area.

In most tax regimes, our client's 'residency status' determines where they must file their primary tax return.

Often, our clients approach us with tax questions concerning how they may effectively cease residency.

Let us consider a recent client example.

Tom was a senior executive for a global company based in Singapore. In 2011, Tom received the good news that he was being promoted to run the company's global business.

The only catch was he had to move into the US tax system. Great news indeed.

Tom had real estate in Australia as well as Singapore.

We had to consider three tax regimes now.

The properties had appreciated in value significantly since Tom bought them.

Under the US tax rules, if Tom moved into the US, he would face significant capital gains tax exposure because the US would not give Tom a 'step up' in the value of the property at the time he entered the US tax system.

Therefore, even though Tom was entering the US tax system with unrealised gains in these properties, he would be taxable on all this gain if he chose to sell them while he was in the US.

This does seem somewhat unfair as this 'pre-migration' gain has had little to do with Tom's US tax residency.

Due to our specialist knowledge of the US, Australian and Singaporean tax systems, we were able to help Tom understand the potential tax exposure and prevent him from triggering a significant tax liability. Indeed, we designed an innovative, thoughtful solution that was, in the end, signed off by the Big 4 firm acting for Tom's employer.

The CST Way is about delivering value and applying our knowledge to our client's facts and circumstances.

There are many examples of people who unwittingly fail to plan and develop a tax strategy around arriving in Expatland and departing their home country.

The importance of tax planning when changing jurisdictions cannot be overemphasised, and there are many potential issues that need to be considered here.

Interaction of Taxation and Legal Systems

In Tom's case, because we had a clear understanding of the potential tax treatment of global assets in the arrival country, we were able to protect Tom from making a very expensive mistake.

Some countries exempt foreign income, others may tax foreign company income on an accruals basis. As a result, many global expats struggle to find a professional tax advisory firm that can provide home country taxation support as well as continuing their services in the arrival country.

CST Tax Advisors has that capability.

We see on a regular basis the adverse consequences of expats unwittingly caught up in the interaction of global tax systems.

Dual Contract or Split Contract Jurisdictions

Several countries, Hong Kong being one example, offer the opportunity for contracts to be structured on the basis that work done in Hong Kong is taxed, whereas work done outside the country is not taxed.

Therefore, where we have clients moving to such jurisdictions, thought is often given as to how employment income can be properly structured.

Double Taxation Agreements

An important aspect of planning for an individual moving to another country is understanding the manner in which the tax laws of both the home country and the arrival country interact.

Globally, there are many bilateral agreements between nations, including Double Taxation Agreements (DTAs) and Taxation Information Exchange Agreements.

These agreements add to the list of factors that need to be addressed to determine the appropriate tax solutions.

As DTAs operate, inter alia, to prevent double taxation, they should always be examined and understood before advising a client on an impending move to Expatland.

An example of the variations that arise from the application of a DTA is seen between Australia and the US, and how capital gains tax is levied in Australia.

If a client is a US resident at the time of the disposal of an asset, there will generally only be tax payable in the US tax system, even if there was no 'exit tax' paid in Australia on that asset. This has major implications regarding decisions made about the asset prior to moving to the US.

Another application of the DTA provisions is through variations in the interest, dividend, and royalty withholding rates between countries. While the base rate for withholding on dividends is 30 per cent, the DTA, however, can vary these amounts to a lower rate such as 15 per cent.

Planning Ahead

Taxation across Expatland is complex as the 'population' is made up of more than 240 million expats of more than 200 nationalities. This leads to the interaction of a multitude of tax and legal systems.

When clients approach us for advice, noting that they are contemplating becoming non-residents, our view is that we need approximately six to twelve months to allow time for appropriate planning. Our client is then given a copy of my first book, Expatland, to read ahead of the move!

There are at least five general legal questions that you should ask when a client is considering a move to Expatland.

These include:

1. What legal system applies in the country that our client is moving to?

2. Is it a civil or common law jurisdiction or perhaps a hybrid legal system?

3. Does the arrival country have a worldwide taxation system?

4. Does the arrival country have a capital gains tax?

5. How does the arrival country treat employee shares and/or stock options?

Avoiding Trouble

Understanding the legal system our clients are moving to is essential.

As a case in point, some countries still operate what may be referred to as 'debtor prisons'. This refers to systems in which people who suffer financial difficulties or owe money to another party through a commercial dispute may be jailed.

Around the time of the 2008 financial crisis, there were many instances of expats leaving their cars at Dubai Airport and flying out to avoid these debtor prisons.

Other countries reserve the right to cancel employment visas in the case of traffic violations.

Understanding the laws in relation to estate planning is also important; for example whether Wills in our clients' home country has legal effect in the country they are heading to.

Some other questions include:

- What is the process required to 'prove' a foreign Will in the arrival country?

- In the case of a loss of mental capacity, does the foreign regime recognise the concept of an 'enduring power of attorney'?

- What inheritance tax is payable on death in the arrival country? Are foreign-held assets included in the inheritance tax base?

Doing it *The CST Way*

- We believe that if we understand our clients' financial position, we will spot opportunities to help them.

- We understand that our clients are not tax advisers and that they rely on us to help them.

- We examine all the records prepared by the client's previous accountant to check what issues lurk within.

- We work collaboratively with related professionals who are part of our client service team.

- We never put in place artificial, contrived or unrealistic steps to achieve a tax outcome.

- We also consider our clients' needs to access capital if some unforeseen eventuality arises.

- We adopt a collaborative approach and we believe in regular contact with our clients.

- Our clients get a copy of *Expatland* before they move.

CHAPTER 5

THE
DEPARTING EXPAT

'Sometimes you need to take a leap of faith from what you do to something that's different in order to find inspiration.' – Tori Amos

Trevor sat in my office in Sydney, 2005. He was at a personal and professional crossroads. His career was stalling in the Australian bank that he was working for. His marriage was under pressure, because he took his work troubles home with him.

It was a year since we had established CST Tax Advisors Singapore.

We were in expansion mode, and although Severe Acute Respiratory Syndrome (SARS) had affected Singapore's economy, we were seeing very good opportunities for the global tax business.

Trevor asked me *'John, do you think I could make a go of it in Singapore?'*

My response was that given the number of expats that had left Singapore recently, I thought that going the other way would make sense.

I invited Trevor to come and stay with me for a few days in Singapore. Trevor explained to his wife, Kristen, that he was going on a fact-finding tour to see what life in Expatland might look like.

It was just the opportunity Trevor was looking for.

Trevor saw 'acres of diamonds' up in Singapore. In 2005, banks in Singapore began hiring. They were looking to replace expats that had left the previous year due to SARS.

Trevor and Kristen, who was also in banking, found great work opportunities in Singapore. Their relationship blossomed and they had their first child, Charlie, in Singapore.

Departing Australia was just the tonic for Trevor.

Taking on the challenge of trying something new is not new. It is done millions of times a year by global expats. But I am sure that in 2005 there would be very few expat couples happier with their move than Trevor and Kristen.

Helping people plan a move to Expatland is second nature to us.

<u>Current tax position</u>

We obtain all relevant information in relation to the client's current financial position on completion of the Fact Finder document. We hold a number of meetings to work through ideas that will help them with their tax and accounting needs in Expatland and their home country.

One example of an issue that frequently arises is the issue of 'exit tax'; that is, the act of leaving one country may trigger the deemed sale of all assets held in their home country. This can have quite serious consequences for the client, so we do need to focus on the issue.

We also consider if any elections are available to retain assets in our client's home country.

The fact that a client is moving to Expatland does not of itself mean that all their assets need to go with them!

For a number of reasons, including family asset protection and risk mitigation, our clients often wish to hold their assets in a third country, through some type of trust.

We practise the delivery of *The CST Way* with flexibility. We can cater to any strategy our client wishes to consider as part of the planning process.

Part of working with empathy for our client is ensuring that a cost benefit analysis is undertaken in relation to any long-term tax, business or accounting strategies so that we can determine if the proposed approach is warranted.

We consider financial and non-financial objectives.

As our clients moving to Expatland usually buy assets in Expatland, we often find ourselves examining the consequences of them moving to a third or fourth country.

Part of our process is to consider how any existing structures owned by our clients are treated when they move to Expatland. Some countries, such as Japan and China, have particularly favourable tax regimes for expats.

As an example, these concessional tax regimes may only tax expats on income arising in Japan or China during the first five years of the expats' tax residence in the country. These transitional rules are generally designed to provide an incentive to work in their country.

Other countries, such as the US, tax expat clients living in the US on passive income accruing in their home country structures.

Our role is to advise our clients about the international tax regime that applies in their arrival country and to help them plan how to deal with these rules.

A good example of a structure that works tax effectively in one jurisdiction, but poorly in another jurisdiction, is an Australian superannuation fund. While they work well in Australia, they are not tax effective in the US. Indeed, the US trust regime can tax gains accruing in an Australian superannuation fund despite the Australian expat not bringing in any of the gains into the US.

We have a number of strategies we can implement to overcome some of these harsh outcomes, but the general message here is plan early and plan often.

Unique residency status

Another factor that must be considered is the type of residency that our clients (the departing expats) will be taking up in their arrival country.

In some circumstances, there are unique residency statuses that can have different tax implications for our client. Examples of this include the 'temporary resident' status in Australia and the 'not ordinary resident' status in Singapore.

Both these types of residency impose different tax outcomes and they can provide some additional flexibility in the tax position of our client relocating to Expatland.

Restructuring

Once we understand our clients' likely residence position in Expatland, then we can plan what to do in relation to any family companies or family trusts they may have.

In some cases, a restructure may only involve changes to the office holders of a company or trustee of a trust.

For example, the residency of the trustee determines the residency status of a trust in Australia. If the intention is to keep the trust a tax resident of Australia, then this may be achieved simply with the resignation of the current trustee (the departing expat) and the appointment of another individual who will remain in Australia.

What can go wrong?

I noted earlier the importance of asking the *What Can Go Wrong Question?*. Let's consider the question further here.

If an expat has left his or her home country and we were not engaged to provide 'exit advice', at no point would we begin preparation of their tax return or provide tax advice until we are clear that all exit issues have been identified. Once identified, the exit issues must then be addressed.

Failure to do so can result in important issues being overlooked. For example, incorrectly recorded 'exit values' of assets held by our client in his or her home country may result in future overpayment of capital gains tax.

Also, issues giving rise to a liability at departure may have been missed with the effect that our client has a liability, which continues to accrue penalty interest. We have often had to break the bad news to clients in Expatland that they still have home country tax liabilities long after they 'left' because they failed to consider a relevant election. That is not a nice conversation to have.

We, therefore, regularly check what work any other previous accountants did in the year of our client's departure. We are very clear about what needs to be done in terms of defining our scope of work for the departing expat.

We take nothing for granted.

Doing it *The CST Way*

- We hold a number of meetings with clients ahead of their move to Expatland.

- We consider what tax elections are available to reduce triggering exit taxes from their home country.

- We perform a cost benefit analysis before we implement strategies to determine if they work favourably for our clients.

- We advise clients about the international tax regime that is waiting for them in Expatland.

- We emphasise the need to plan early.

- We always check what departure tax advice our clients received.

CHAPTER 6

THE ARRIVING EXPAT

"Exploration is the engine that drives innovation. Innovation drives economic growth. So, let's all go exploring.' – Edith Widder

The thrill of arriving in a new location and getting 'business ready' is an experience that one must experience to truly understand. Having done that now in many countries, I can tell you that no two arrivals are the same.

There are new challenges, new pitfalls, and new opportunities around every corner.

The arriving expat must have resilience or else the unpredictable nature of the challenges will soon have them on the plane home!

Our job is to make their life easier when it comes to dealing with their tax and accounting needs.

Sometimes, however, people assume that arriving in Expatland has no consequences (without talking to us!) and that can make things difficult for us.

A recent example springs to mind.

David Smith, an expat relocating from Singapore to the US (upon his retirement), decided to access his Australian superannuation fund.

What a mistake that was.

In Australia, pension payments for those over 60 years of age are tax free.

This is, however, not the case in the US.

David had worked out that he and his wife, Annette, could afford to live in the US the way they envisaged, based on paying no US federal or state tax.

They were quite shocked when we told them that the US would tax David's Australian-sourced pension stream.

As we will discuss below, there are many things to think about when one arrives in Expatland.

The tax issues associated with arriving in Expatland are as numerous as those related to departing their home country.

Generally, the issues that need to be considered can include some or all of the following:
- complying with the requirements of more than one tax jurisdiction

- accounting for a new tax and legal system

- understanding the tax issues associated with moving to the arrival country

- considering how foreign assets are accounted for

- locating other professional service providers to work with.

As one of our competitive advantages, our principals work on clients' issues together in 'real time' to provide integrated and consistent advice.

Arrival into Expatland

When our client re-enters their home country, there are many tax implications that must be considered.

Their arrival must be carefully planned as the ramifications of an ill-prepared arrival can be costly for our client. In many jurisdictions, our clients may be deemed to have acquired all their assets for their fair market value at the date of their arrival.

This information will often differ from the cost of the assets and such details must be kept for many years until the asset is eventually sold.
Establishing new connections and services

When a client arrives in Expatland, we can play a role in assisting them with establishing connections with other financial service providers, including financial planners, and other legal and banking professionals.

We use this team approach when working with complementary professionals to ensure our clients' needs are addressed across all areas related to their tax and financial management.

Management of client expectations and communication

The majority of our clients are unaware of the many tax issues associated with moving and relocating.

Therefore, we ensure they obtain and read a copy of my book, Expatland. This book helps them understand the variety of taxation, legal and family issues to consider.

Our clients appreciate that a single country tax system is generally comprehensive and complicated enough and that the level of complexity only increases when they have to deal with two or more jurisdictions.

Doing it *The CST Way*

- We know that the tax issues associated with arriving in Expatland are as many as those related to departing their home country.

- Our principals work on clients together in 'real time' to provide integrated and consistent advice.

- When a client arrives in Expatland, we play a role in assisting them with establishing connections with other financial service professionals.

- We use this team approach working with complementary professionals to ensure our clients' needs are addressed across all areas related to their tax and financial management.

CHAPTER 7

THE FIRST-UP MEETING FOR PRIVATE CLIENTS

'The travel, the amazing work I have had the chance to do, the meetings with different people are all very inspiring and give me lots of positive energy.' - Saskia de Brauwr

Sitting at the Wanderers Stadium in Johannesburg on 17 April 2009 and watching the Australian cricketers play South Africa in a day/night match might not sound like your typical first-up client meeting, but that is what it was for me. I was working through some key issues with Maggie, the chief financial officer (CFO) of a South African retail business looking to expand to Australia.

Maggie wanted to gain a better understanding of the Australian tax system and the rates of withholding tax in relation to profits distributed to South Africa..

The challenge for me was that Australia was batting and I love cricket about as much as I love tax!

While covering the general points about the Australian tax system, we did take a brief pause in our discussions to watch Michael Clarke as he built his impressive innings.

Maggie was not as much of a cricket fan as I was and she was at the cricket as part of a corporate hospitality event put on by her employer and the company owner, Neil. Therefore, having a 'first-up' meeting with me at the cricket was a great way for Maggie to assess both our technical capabilities as a firm and also my dedication to helping my clients.

As the match got closer and more exciting (happily Australia won!), I had to ask for a brief suspension of our first-up meeting. Thankfully, Maggie agreed and our first-up moved to her office the next day.

Now typically the first-up meeting does not happen at an international cricket match, but this was one of those occasions.

I had proved my dedication to the task and we ended up having a great client relationship.

My golden rule is that if at the end of the first-up we do not get a real sense of being able to (or wanting to) help the potential client, then we go no further.

We are not obligated to deal with clients who we do not want to help.

Now, let us look at the 'first-up' more closely.

The 'First-Up' meeting

The first-up meeting with our prospective client is the foundation in establishing a relationship with him or her.

It also allows us work out if we are able to help him or her.

It is a great opportunity to convey our abilities with being able to assess and resolve any tax, accounting and business advisory challenges that arise.

The first-up client meeting is also our earliest opportunity to understand their personal and financial objectives, the location of their assets, their income streams, and other important information.

We ask the *R-Factor Question®* and the *What Can Go Wrong Question?*.

On some occasions, it becomes apparent that our client is looking for a broad range of tax accounting and business advisory services. In other situations, a private client is looking for the delivery of focused tax compliance services.

In all cases, without a completed Fact Finder document and without asking the two key questions, we will be unable to fully understand our client's position.

When a prospective client seeks our services or reaches out to a professional at CST Tax Advisors, generally we engage them via one of our principals.

Only our principals have the complete international experience to effectively assess the range of services our client may need. This also extends to cases where clients require interaction with a foreign CST Tax Advisors office. It is our principals, working together across borders, who deliver client solutions.

The CST Way is, whenever possible, to have a face-to-face meeting with our client. As noted earlier, the 'whiteboard session' (originally named because we used four electronic whiteboards) is a terrific bonding experience. The whiteboard session considers our client's assets, liabilities, income and expenses along with their objectives.

An alternative to the face-to-face meeting could be a Skype call for those global expats residing in locations where we do not have a CST Tax Advisors office.

The least favoured option is the international teleconference, but indeed sometimes Skype conferences are not possible and we have to make do with what we have available.

At our meeting, our first approach is to draw a pie chart divided into the following five segments:

1. tax planning and compliance
2. insurance review
3. investment review
4. superannuation and pension review
5. trust and legal review.

The following diagram shows the model in action.

This method provides our client with a visual understanding of how we can help them along *The CST Way*.

Let us discuss each of the above segments of the pie.

a) Tax planning and compliance

As part of the core offering, we consider what tax-planning issues arise and how to implement our ideas.

We have already analysed our client's Fact Finder, understood the *R-Factor Question®* and the *What Can Go Wrong Question?*.

We now have the information we need to do this work.

b) Investment review

We are not wealth advisers or financial planners. That said, we do work with complementary professionals and we consider understanding our clients' investments central to our role. Where the clients have invested and the types of income streams they earn is very important to the '*Tax compliance and planning*' piece of the pie.

It may be that our clients are not happy with how they are being advised in these areas. We can introduce them to wealth advisers and private bankers with whom we have worked and trust.

c) *Insurance review*

Interestingly, there are quite a few different tax outcomes related to insurance. Hence, knowing what insurances our clients have and what risks they are protecting is vital to this process.

For example, a family business client may hold a life insurance policy in a trading company to cover some 'keyperson risk'. In Australia, this would mean that any payout would be taxable.

Now, a better way of holding this insurance would be if the life insurance is held in a purpose-designed insurance trust and then any proceeds can be structured on a tax-free basis.

The basic lesson is that if we do not review what insurances our clients hold and how they hold them, then things can and will be missed.

It is also likely that we will involve an insurance specialist to conduct a review of what our client has and/or needs. While we are not insurance specialists, this does not mean we do not help when we can.

d) Trust and legal review

Any review of a client's affairs and how to help him or her must include a *Trust and legal review*.

Essential questions here are:

• Does our client have a family trust?

It is important to know how assets are held.

• Have we read the trust deed?

The trust deed may be an 'off-the-shelf deed' which has not kept pace with tax laws. We may need to review it or have key terms amended.

• Is the deed properly signed and completed?

It is amazing how sometimes a signed deed cannot be found! This would call for a solution in many other ways that are beyond the scope of this book.

• Does our client have a Will? If not, this becomes a high priority!

It is very important to know how our client's assets would pass among the family in the event of an untimely demise.

- Is our client a director in some companies we do not know about?

This is an essential question given that we consider how our client's personal assets might be exposed to litigation.

There is a lot of risk around being a company director for a trading business these days, so making sure client assets are not exposed is something that we do.

- If our client does not have a trust, should they?

Clearly, an important part of helping clients manage their taxes is thinking about how they hold them in the first place!

It may be that a trust is a good option for both tax and asset protection.

In addressing some of these questions, we work with lawyers we know and trust in various jurisdictions to solve some of the above questions.

e) Superannuation and pension review

We need to understand our client's superannuation position and how he or she is accumulating funds for their retirement.

Given the client's age and profile, it may be apparent to us that they have more opportunities in this area to obtain tax deductions by making contributions here.

Where required by the laws of various countries, we can bring in financial advisers that specialise in this work to join us in helping our clients.

We view our role as 'quarterback' for our clients.

We believe that by working through the above process we can coordinate all these pieces of the pie for our clients. We can help them find complementary professionals to assist as needed.

Using a circle diagram is a great visual aid.

Once our clients see how we view their financial position, they immediately understand that we are more than accountants who just focus on traditional 'tax compliance and accounting'.

They understand that *The CST Way* is unique.

Our view is that if we do not look to be involved in assisting our clients with respect of their overall financial and tax management objectives (and indeed take on the responsibility to be involved where we can), we will miss the broader issues that can affect our clients' tax, business, and accounting needs.

As a result, we would fail to 'empathise' properly with their facts and circumstances as they change over time.

This focus distinguishes us from other firms that operate on a global basis.

More on the 'first-up'

Operating in a reactive way at arm's length from a client and simply proceeding on a question-and-answer basis is not *The CST Way*. Up close and personal is *The CST Way*. We believe in getting to the heart of our client's needs and objectives.

As such, we usually request copies of our client's previous tax returns ahead of the first-up meeting.

Our view is that reviewing a client's previous tax returns is a good way of developing some contextual knowledge of what tax issues may lurk within our client's tax affairs.

Where our client is married or has a partner, usually we request that their spouse or partner attend the first-up meeting.

This gives us a sense of how the couple cooperates in relation to their financial affairs.

There is little point in going through the 'circle process' outlined above with only 50 per cent of the decision makers present!

There have been many times when I have seen only one of the couple and then I have subsequently found out that we have only covered less than half the issues affecting the family.

The key lesson here is that we aim to work with couples as we 'go around the circle'.

Their combined responses to the *R-Factor Question*® and the *What Can Go Wrong Question?* are what we need.

Following the first-up meeting, we have a great record of all the information gained through the process. We have a clear pathway forward.

We accept clients if they possess the following attributes:

- They are within our areas of client focus.
- They are respectful of our services and knowledge.
- They are ready to pay our quoted fees.
- They understand and value what we are doing for them.

Non-acceptance of a prospective client

From the principals' perspective, when introduced to a prospective client, we ensure that we have the necessary expertise to undertake our client service. If at the end of the first-up meeting there is little prospect that we can add further value to our client, we generally do not engage with them.

Our business is a personal one.

Therefore, from the outset, there must be mutual respect, trust and understanding.

There must be a shared vision between our client and the CST Tax Advisors team or we cannot accept the appointment.

Doing it *The CST Way*

- The first-up meeting with a prospective client is the basis upon which we build a long-term client relationship.

- It is our first opportunity to understand our client's financial position.

- Wherever possible the first-up is face to face.

- An alternative to the face to face could be a Skype session if the client lives in a country where we do not have an office.

- We view our role as our client's quarterback.

- Our view is that if we do not get involved with assisting our clients in the spectrum of their tax and financial management objectives, we will miss the broader issues that can affect their tax, business and accounting needs.

- One of our beliefs is that if our client service team is not committed to helping a particular individual for personality or other reasons, we do not engage with that prospective client.

CHAPTER 8

OUR
BUSINESS TAX PLANS

**'Those who fail to plan, plan to fail.' –
Winston Churchill**

*While having lunch with one of my clients, Rajesh, in
Singapore, the topic of US expansion came up. Rajesh was
the chief marketing officer (CMO) for a film production
company. I said this sounded great and I wanted to know
what it meant for him. He said it was early days, but the
chief executive officer (CEO) 'had it covered'.*

The following day I met Robin, the CEO, with a view
to seeing if we could provide some US– Singapore
tax advice. I was amazed to hear Robin proclaim

that the company had recently expanded to the US, leased an office, but had yet to do a business plan or a cash flow forecast!

The company expected to establish a business in Hollywood for under US$10m.

Robin expressed confidence that the company's impeccable front-end connections with agents, producers and film distributors would generate a lot of demand for their Asian product.

They had done little preparation in terms of a US business tax plan and the likely impact of the US federal and state taxes on their US income, or the impact of withholding taxes on profit repatriations to Singapore.

Shortly after my meeting with Robin, the company listed its business in Singapore.

Two years and US$30m later, the company went into liquidation. I was far from surprised.

While we were engaged to advise some of the key executives about their personal US tax, we did not act for the company. That privilege went to a Big 4 firm.

That Big 4 firm managed to overlook advising the Board of Directors that a business plan –including the impact of taxes – would have shown that the entertainment company was running an unsustainable business model.

As we discuss below, our approach is radically different.

When we are approached to act as chartered accountants for a client who wishes to expand globally, we ensure that we have read their business plan.

Our approach

It is important to note, however, that although we are qualified chartered accountants, our primary expertise is in taxation planning and compliance, not management consulting.

Often, we can be an important sounding board on non-tax issues.

Sometimes we make a referral to a business coach, a business specialist or a management consultant if our client would like further help with their business plan.

It is also important for us to understand if our client has the necessary financial resources to execute their business plan. Failure to do this can create problems dealing with tax payments later on.

A good question to ask in the case of start-up businesses is how much the client is prepared to put in funding to reach a break-even point. Hesitancy in the reply or no real idea might indicate we will not have our client for long!

Other relevant questions to consider are:

- Is the business a business that we understand?

- Do we understand the reporting requirements our client is seeking?

- Is our client able to assess properly how their business is performing?

From the perspective of designing a future tax strategy, we need to consider through which sort of structure our client might operate the business? Is it a partnership, trust or other corporate body?

Our client should understand their key performance indicators (KPIs) in the relevant industry.

One of our primary concerns is the protection of our client and their personal assets.

Often, this involves segregating risk.

Role of the tax plan

Having understood the business plan, we then turn our mind towards the tax plan.

As noted in the previous section, the tax plan is a subset of the business plan.

We frequently use the analogy that tax is the tail of the fox, not the head of the fox! This means that tax planning follows the strategic plan of the business.

We know that a business should not be designed around a tax plan.

Against that background, when looking at a global tax plan, there are three key steps to consider:

1. *Ensure that tax treaties in relation to foreign countries affecting the tax plan are identified and understood.*

2. *Ensure that there are appropriate skills and expertise in relation to tax accounting and legal professionals in the countries as these are of prime importance to our clients as their international structure is put together.*

There is little point is selecting a jurisdiction if the professionals' skill base, the available information technology (IT) infrastructure and the banking and legal system do not meet acceptable global standards.

3. *Ensure that the tax plan is capable of being modified and adapted depending on business outcomes.*

In one recent case, we were asked to act for a potential client in the clothing industry that expanded to the US. When we investigated behind the scenes, we found that the potential client expanded to the US without realising the enormous costs involved.

They failed to understand the all the tax issues associated with moving to the US. They then suffered the consequences of horrendous failures to plan at both a tax and business level. In the end, the Australian business was essentially funding the failed US business and our client had to withdraw from the US market.

The potential client moved first then thought later.

When they asked us to 'rescue' them from the many tax issues that came up, many years had already passed for us to help effectively following the decline.

Any tax plan we design that deals with transactions between related parties must also consider the potential exposure of transfer pricing legislation.

As noted earlier, the philosophy of *The CST Way* is to work collaboratively with fellow specialists who possess skills we do not. This is generally the case with transfer pricing.

Further considerations

There are many things to consider when designing a tax plan for a global client, including the impact of local legislation on principals or directors of the relevant CST Tax Advisors office.

We are always mindful of our obligations to the tax authorities of the relevant country.

We endeavour to ensure that our client's international expansion plans are cognisant of all their tax obligations in various jurisdictions.

We are a global tax practice and our clients expand globally.

Generally, we do not act for a client in terms of helping them expand from one location to the other, unless we understand who our client uses for professional tax and accounting in their home country.

If we are approached to provide international tax advice, but we have not previously acted for our client and we have no knowledge of who their current advisers are, we do not accept the appointment without making it clear that we need to work with their existing professionals.

An example occurred recently where a client came to our Singapore office seeking tax advice between

Australia and Singapore. We indicated to our client that we would not be providing advice in a vacuum, and in the absence of a working relationship with their Australian tax advisers, we would not accept the engagement.

Our client was surprised to hear this.

However, while that may have seemed strange to our client, advising them without knowing the full facts of their Australian position and the issues affecting their tax position in Australia would have been inconsistent with our professional approach.

We do not see the merit of a foreign CST Tax Advisors office providing international advice to a resident of another country unless the 'home country' accountant is signing off on the domestic consequences and is aware of our role.

If we are not the domestic accountants for our client, then we must work with the professional accountant who is.

If the domestic accountant for the particular client does not have the skill set to expand overseas, we can accept the appointment, but only on the basis that our comments are shared with the domestic accountant so that they understand what we are suggesting and are happy to work collaboratively with us.

Once completed, the global tax plan is a document that is often referred to by a variety of individuals across the globe. It contains all the advice provided to our client and the way such advice is to be implemented.

As part of our analysis, we often prepare cash flows showing the impact the new entities make on our client's global financial and cash position.

Our global tax plans are premium documents and often can take some time to put together, depending upon the complexity inherent in the matter.

As we act as the quarterback for our client with regards to their global tax affairs on many occasions, we work with external tax advisers and legal advisers to pull together the required tax legal, structuring, and accounting solutions.

This separates CST Tax Advisors from many other tax and accounting firms.

Doing it *The CST Way*

- We work with our clients to check that they have the necessary financial resources to execute their business plan.

- We are able to refer our clients to a wide variety of management consultants or business consultants depending on their needs as they enter the foreign market.

- We believe that the protection of our client and their assets is a key concern.

- We know that a business plan should not be designed around a tax plan.

- We are mindful of our obligations to the tax offices of the countries in which our clients do business.

- We do not act for a client in terms of helping them move around the globe unless we know who their accountants and lawyers currently are.

- We look at the impact of taxation on their international business cash flows.

CHAPTER 9

SERVICE
AND INTEGRITY

'To give real service, you must add something which
cannot be bought or measured with money, and
that is sincerity and integrity.' – Douglas Adams

*It was 6 March 1993 and my client Peter, who was heading
overseas on a break, asked me to sell some of his stock in a
company listed on the Australian Stock Exchange (as it
was formerly called) within a certain price range.*

As I had Peter's power of attorney, I could easily
instruct a broker to do this trade. I called a
broker who worked for a well-known boutique
Australian investment bank. I had clients who

worked there and I believed it would be done in a straightforward manner.

How wrong I was.

I had instructed the broker to sell the stock within a price range, but for some unexplained reason not only did the broker not complete the order, but she went home before market close and without passing the order on to someone to cover it for her.

The next morning the stock opened down and my client, Peter, was looking at a A$36,000 loss.

Peter was less than pleased when I told him.

I approached the bank to cover it. They refused, citing it as not their problem. Their view was that I was not specific and I should have kept an eye on the trade and called back in before market close to check on the order.

Given I would not accept losing Peter as my client, I had two choices: I could sue the bank or I could fund it myself.

I chose the second option.

The CST Way is about service and integrity.

It is about putting your hand up when you make a mistake.

Unlike the bank, which I found out later quietly sacked the stockbroker concerned, I owned the business and the buck stopped with me.

I was not going to lose a client due to the bank's incompetence.

However, this was a good lesson for me.

In choosing people to work with my clients, from that time on, I would only choose related professionals that have sincerity and integrity based on our dealings with them.

I knew that there were many things that my international private clients would need, including legal services, private banking, immigration, broking and financial planning, just to name a few.

The 'share broking lesson' made me appreciate the need to choose referral partners wisely.

The follow-up to the above story was that Peter was so impressed with my acceptance of the mistake, my sincerity and integrity, that he and his family group stayed with me for many more years.

I earned that $36,000 back many times over.

We are now very specific about the range of services we provide clients and how we vet our referral team.

To become a member of our complementary client service team, we conduct due diligence on potential members and we go through a process.

This includes:

1. an introductory meeting to understand the client's service delivery process
2. a walk through their internal operating system
3. a review of all their collateral documents and marketing material
4. entry into a service delivery standard agreement for our clients: do's and don'ts
5. a quarterly review of cases we are mutually working on.

We believe strongly in 'face-to-face' meetings with people in our complementary service provider referral team.

Over time the relationship evolves and trust increases.

We believe that regular communication is essential between complementary service providers so that issues do not fall through the cracks.

As noted earlier, our main service for individual clients is the provision of taxation advice and compliance services. We assist our clients comply with tax residency laws.

Regardless of where a client is heading to or arriving from, we assist them with both their local and international tax needs.

In those jurisdictions where we do not have a CST Tax Advisors office, we make connections with fellow taxation service providers and in areas beyond taxation services. As noted above, my book Expatland discusses a range of additional matters that our clients will need to address and consider.

The specialist advice aspect of our practice is often why clients come to CST Tax Advisors and why *The CST Way* has a lot of potency in terms of the strategies and the creative solutions we employ.

We often hear praise from our clients as to how uncommon it is for an accounting firm to cover tax solutions for both the home country and the arrival country.

This is very rewarding and gratifying for all of us at CST Tax Advisors.

We take great pride in being our clients' first point of call when they need professional advice.

Doing it *The CST Way*

- The CST Way is about sincerity and integrity.

- We are accountable for our performance and accept responsibility for any errors we make.

- We are very specific about the related service providers with whom we work.

- We are careful and thorough in how we vet them.

- We believe in face-to-face meetings with people in our complementary service provider referral team.

- We make connections with fellow taxation service providers and in areas beyond taxation services in those jurisdictions where we do not have a CST Tax Advisors office.

CHAPTER 10

THE PRIVATE CLIENT TAX RETURN

'The hardest thing to understand in the world is the income tax.' - Albert Einstein

At 9am, I arrived at the Luxe Hotel on Rodeo Drive, Beverly Hills, on 11 March 2009 on a bright Saturday morning. I was due to meet an Australian client that had recently moved to Newport. We did not, at the stage, have an office in the US and I was beginning to look at the US market given the numbers of expats that moved to the US each year.

Ahead my first meeting, I thought that reading the instructions for a US Form 1040 could not be that hard and it would provide me with useful background information for the meeting I was about to have.

Only then did the above quote from Einstein hit me like a brick!

The concept of the Alternative Minimum Tax (AMT) filled me with a mix of confusion and amusement. I found it surprising that you could have no actual income, yet Uncle Sam could tax you anyway!

Only in America, I thought.

As I drank my third coffee of the morning, I was comforted by the thought that any expat in the US would face a similar uphill battle doing their own 1040s. The complexity of the language in the explanation booklet meant a new international tax practice would surely thrive in the US.

By the time our client left that morning, I realised that we had no time to lose to establish an office in Los Angeles. Today, we have four US offices and more are on the way.

What I have since come to appreciate is that the Internal Revenue Service (IRS) collects an inordinate amount of data, not only from the income tax return, but also other forms such as the Report of Foreign

Bank and Financial Accounts (FBAR), the Form 3520, the Form 8938 and many more forms.

Having to prepare and lodge income tax returns in your home country and in the US is a complex exercise, and given the amount of information shared on a global basis between revenue authorities, having private client tax returns prepared by a trained professional is essential.

In the many countries in which we operate, the individual tax return forms the key compliance document for our client. The importance of this document cannot be overstated.

Indeed, a prominent Australian tax counsel frequently cites a tax return as 'a client's testament to the Commissioner'. That being the case, we must understand very carefully what our client is 'testifying to'.

We understand that a client's tax return conveys data and intelligence that will be used by one or more revenue authorities to form a picture of his or her life. It allows these revenue authorities to look at outliers and consider which clients are worthy of further review. We review the information that goes into the tax return carefully.

In the case of family members, inconsistencies between their income returns can lead to needless enquiries by the revenue authorities.

For example, 'merely' omitting to change a residential address from the Australian address to the foreign address can result in the Australian Taxation Office having the erroneous view that a client has not changed residency or has a different residence from their spouse.

We assist our clients in their home country and their arrival country with the preparation of their income tax returns.

In this regard, the tax residence of an individual forms the foundation stone as to the nature of the information that is required in order for CST Tax Advisors to complete a tax return engagement.

As an example, where our client is a resident of Australia, then he/she will generally be required to declare his or her income received during the year from worldwide sources.

The CST Way ensures that our professionals only proceed to complete client work if it makes sense to them. This means that incomplete data or sources of income that are not clear will not form part of any work we do. None of our professionals begin working on something that they do not understand.

Our preparation and review processes ensure that the highest possible quality tax returns are prepared and presented to our clients.

Doing it *The CST Way*

- In the many countries in which we operate, the individual tax return forms the key compliance document for our client

- We understand that a client's tax return conveys data and intelligence that will be used by one or more revenue authorities to form a picture of his or her life and we review that information very carefully.

- We assist our clients in their home country and their arrival country with the preparation of their income tax returns.

- The CST Way ensures that our professionals only proceed to complete client work if it makes sense to them.

CHAPTER 11

COMPANY TAX MANAGEMENT AND PLANNING

'So, every dollar of income that I have that is potentially taxed away is a dollar I can't put in my company to create a job. My entire company is centred around job creation.' – Curt Schilling

Sitting at the Marriott Café at the JW Marriott, Hong Kong, in October 2007, Brian mentioned to me that he had been contacted in London by the Economic Development Board (EDB) of Singapore and asked to establish a subsidiary of his UK-based business in Singapore. Brian had founded his shipbroking company ten years earlier and built it up to employ over 150 people.

Brian explained that he was interested primarily, because the tax incentives on offer in Singapore coupled with the sound business environment were very attractive.

I marvelled at the EDB's approach.

They had sourced Brian's businesses in the UK as one they wanted to see expand and relocate to Singapore. As 'first-up' meetings go, this was a terrific opportunity. We received the full mandate to establish the Singapore subsidiary of Brian's business in Singapore.

It was before the financial crisis and shipping profits were still quite high. Over subsequent weeks, the EDB facilitated us gaining access to many tax and business incentives for Brian's company.

I should say just a few words on Singapore. Singapore is an excellent jurisdiction in which to do business. The government is responsive and business focused, and Singapore makes a genuine effort to attract inward investment in those industries in which it sees a competitive advantage for the country.

Over the ensuring years, Brian's company has created many jobs for Singapore's economy and his company became recognised in Asia Pacific.

Our success in helping Brian with the relocation of his company, tax management and business planning brought home to us all at CST Tax Advisors that assisting companies expand in Expatland is both professionally rewarding and something we have a unique competence in.

We have since developed a specialisation in working with companies looking for competitive business and tax regimes.

Broader role

While our primary role as tax advisers to our business clients is to assist them with the management and planning of their company tax affairs, we often do more than that. Among the many things we do for our clients, we also assess their tax risk and help them manage that risk.

We ensure that we communicate often with them in relation to a variety of issues, including the timing of tax payments, and other businesses and tax issues that may impact them.

As many of our clients have family-owned businesses, there are often personal issues that can affect the corporate tax plan. A couple of examples involve family disputes over deceased estates or family law issues relating to marriage dissolution.

We design our corporate tax plans to be flexible enough to adapt to external adverse issues affecting the family group.

Thinking about the company and ignoring what is going on in the lives of the major shareholders is not The CST Way. We understand that there is no 'one-size-fits-all' solution to efficient and effective tax management. Each business client has his or her own unique needs with different expectations as to how to allocate resources, manage risk and generate business value.

We believe that identifying issues early is the key to efficient tax management and planning.

An example of an unexpected tax liability occurred recently to a new client of ours. The client is in the dental industry. Our client had several domestic and international practices and it was in acquisition mode.

In the year prior to becoming a CST Tax Advisors client, our client had bought three dental practices in Asia. While the first two practices were tax compliant, the third had undisclosed tax liabilities. Our client was liable for the past tax debts of this practice.

The lawyer advising on the purchase of the third practice was not 'tax aware' and he had not ensured that a satisfactory 'tax indemnity' was in the share purchase agreement.

The company tax return

The preparation of a company tax return is one of our key service offerings. The income tax return conveys key information to the relevant tax revenue office, which is used to compare that company with other companies in the same business.

We find it very helpful in preparing a tax return to review and understand the company's financial statements.

It is not *The CST Way* to prepare a company tax return unless we have prepared the financial statements for our client, or we are very confident that a qualified accountant has prepared them. We ensure we understand all account balances.

In many countries, the company tax return is used for statistical purposes and benchmarking in order to select audit targets. Thus, it is essential that it is carefully prepared.

Clients often do not appreciate how the information in the tax return may disclose red flag issues within their business. This could be anything from the ratio of sales to interest, which may be out of line for companies in the same business, or the continual build-up of tax losses year after year.

Therefore, it is incumbent upon us to analyse the information in the client return and look at what seems unusual so we can raise it with our client. We are always prepared for any enquiries we may receive from any global tax authority because company tax returns that we prepare are fully supported by external *'client-source information'*.

In undertaking our compliance work, we always hold true to the key principle of *The CST Way*, which is passion for tax combined with accountability for our performance.

Doing it *The CST Way*

- We have developed a specialisation in working with companies looking for competitive business and tax regimes.

- We assess our client's tax risk and help them manage it.

- We design our corporate tax plans to be flexible enough to adapt to external adverse issues affecting the family group.

- We believe that identifying issues early is the key to efficient tax management and planning.

- We do not prepare a company tax return unless we have either prepared the financial statements or we are very confident that a qualified accountant prepared the financial statements, and we understand all account balances.

- We are always prepared for any enquiries we may receive from any global tax authority, because company tax returns that are prepared by us are fully supported by external 'client-source information'.

CHAPTER 12

COMPANIES HEADING TO EXPATLAND

'No idea for a new growth business ever comes fully shaped. When it emerges, it's half-baked, and it then goes through a process of becoming fully shaped.' – Clayton M. Christensen

22 November 2002 was an auspicious day. It was my 38th birthday, and as my family and I flew out of Melbourne on QF9 bound for London on our year-long sabbatical, I knew that (to paraphrase the X-files) my future was out there.

A few months before, feeling somewhat jaded and knowing things were not quite right, I sensed that I needed time away to think, relax and give myself time to plan.

I needed to discover the next leg of the CST journey.

Indeed, my firm was not called CST Tax Advisors at that point. Our firm was still trading as Marcarian & Co. Lots of ideas would stream into my head over the ensuing year and a name change was just one of them.

There was a big wide world out there and it occurred to me that international tax was the glue that touched almost every business transaction. Also, every expat client had to deal with multiple tax issues at some stage or another.

Now focused on an emerging vision, I made it my business to visit most of the European tax jurisdictions, including Luxembourg, Liechtenstein, Cyprus and Guernsey. I also travelled around Switzerland discovering the cantons of Geneva, Lugarno, Zurich, Zug and others. It was interesting to discover that each canton actively competed against the other by offering tax incentives to attract new residents.

During this marvellous year, I met many private bankers and found out what made them tick and how they dealt with global clients demanding international tax solutions.

Driving around Europe with no fixed itinerary gave me plenty of time for contemplation (not to mention it was great time to write poetry!).

It was without doubt, time was the most significant period of my life in terms of free time to think.

As the quote says, my idea about CST Tax Advisors was not fully formed.

Over the course of the year, I went back to my beginnings and re-examined what brought me into tax in the first place. I knew that my passion for international tax was enduring and was undiminished. However, I knew that only operating from an Australian base would not lead to the growth I wanted for my business.

I knew we needed to be global.

I also felt strongly that integrating and solving global tax problems for expats and businesses moving around would be an area where our business could excel. It was the way of the future.

Upon my return to Australia in late 2003, I headed to Singapore and Hong Kong to observe the expat market, speak to service providers and people I knew. Over the next few months, I went about getting ready to expand our business overseas.

I took the Kevin Costner approach to business building from the movie *Field of Dreams*. That approach was along the lines of the famous quote in the movie *'If you build it, he will come'*. Except in our case it was *'If you set up an office in Singapore, our clients will come'*.

And come they did.

No other chartered accounting firm was operating between Australia and Singapore.

We soon expanded our offering to Hong Kong.

Our local presence and our ability to solve problems across the spectrum of tax and accounting was a distinct advantage in the marketplace.

We moved quickly, employing local people, and joining business groups to expand market awareness of our service offering.

We promoted our business to related service providers, banks, law firms and relocation companies.

In the high growth period prior to 2008, we capitalised on our 'first mover advantage' and we gained many new Australian and other expat clients. Expanding overseas in markets where we had no effective competition was the right move for us at the right time.

Since 2004, we have broadened our offering and moved beyond the Australian-only focus of our business.

We assist our clients with managing a number of common risks as they expand into foreign markets including:

- the real financial cost of expansion

- the cultural divide between domestic and foreign markets

- regulatory differentials between domestic and foreign markets.

We give them a copy of my book, *Expatland.*

As one of the few global firms that understands taxation in Expatland from both a private client and an entrepreneur's perspective, we provide our clients with unparalleled services and access to our related professional service providers through our global networks.

As our professionals are all part of one unified team working The CST Way, we have a distinct advantage when servicing our global clients.

When working with clients heading overseas, we cover many areas relating to setting up their business. Some of these areas are discussed below.

Setting up business

We generally work with our clients for between six and twelve months before they head overseas.

We help clients make sure that when they pay tax overseas, it can be credited in their home country when profits are remitted. Sometimes the best country to pay tax in is where the majority of shareholders live. This is so that shareholders might be able to get a credit for tax paid by the company.

Foreign tax paid at the company level is generally not something that shareholders in another country get a tax credit for.

We help our clients decide on the best form of business structure also. In our experience, while the main forms of business entities can vary from country to country, those countries with English common law regimes, generally have similar types of structures.

Many countries have structures that provide limited liability to owners, but are treated as 'flow-through' vehicles for tax purposes, so only the owners are taxed. A classic example is a US LLC (limited liability company).

We bring our focus to the key issues to consider on departure. The key issues are discussed below.

Issue 1: How does the foreign country tax system work?

In a number of countries, the US being a prime example, there can often be three levels of tax. For example, in New York, there is federal tax, state tax and city tax to contend with. In other countries like Hong Kong, foreign income is exempt from tax.

Issue 2: Transfer pricing issues

We help clients identify transfer-pricing issues.

Recently, a prospective client in the global travel business told us that they had a 'back office' for their IT department in San Francisco. They then told us that their previous accountant had told them they did not have to worry about filing a US tax return – because the branch was not charging any expenses back to Australia and they were just covering their direct costs!

Great news, they thought, until we had to tell them that it was totally incorrect.

Upon a review of the facts of the case, it actually turned out that they had a 'permanent establishment' in the US. This gave them a US tax filing obligation.

The previous accountant also completely missed that transfer pricing rules demand that a market price be charged by the San Francisco office to the head office for the services being provided to head office.

Our client had no idea about these issues.

This is one of the challenges we regularly face when dealing with clients coming to us from domestic-only focused firms.

Firms that focus only on single country tax systems with little or no expertise in international tax, nonetheless, often seek to advise clients going overseas. Rather than admitting 'they don't know what they don't know' and looking to work with a specialist firm to get some outside help, they try to do it in-house.

Usually, this leads to expensive mistakes.

Issue 3: Using debt or equity to fund the foreign expansion

In using capital to start a foreign business, one of the key issues to consider is how to get money into the foreign operation and then how to get profits out.

Many financial controllers take the view that lending money into the foreign business is easier because it can be 'repaid' with little or no complexity. The general thought is that money that goes in as a loan can come out as a loan, right? Well it is not always that simple.

Many foreign countries have rules that require the payment of interest on inter-company loans.

Issue 4: How to send profits to the home country

Having considered how to fund the foreign business and make it profitable, the next question we think about for our clients is how profits can be remitted to their home country.

There are a number of techniques that can be used to send profits home. These include dividends, interest, or royalty payments. Other techniques include management fees and head office recharge. One of the issues to consider here, includes the likely imposition of a foreign withholding tax on payments out of the country.

Doing it *The CST Way*

- We assist our clients with managing a number of common risks as they expand into foreign markets, including:
  - the real financial cost of expansion
  - the cultural divide between domestic and foreign markets
  - regulatory differentials between domestic and foreign markets.

- We provide our clients with unparalleled service and access to our related professional service providers in our global networks.

- We generally work with our clients for between six and twelve months before they head overseas.

- We help our clients decide on the optimal business structure for their activities.

- We bring our focus to bear on considering key issues such as:
  - operation of the foreign tax system
  - transfer pricing
  - using debt or equity to fund the business
  - how to send profits to the home country.

CHAPTER 13

Companies Arriving In Expatland

'The shortest and surest way of arriving at real knowledge is to unlearn the lessons we have been taught, to mount the first principles, and take nobody's word about them.' – Henry Bolingbroke

'We don't do things that way' was what the US-based CFO told me when I suggested they get an arm's-length review of their 'global transfer pricing model' by an Australian transfer pricing specialist.

The company, let's call them 'CabinetMaker Inc.', was supplying IT products and services from the US to Australia.

They decided that the Australian company would, 'just like all other overseas subsidiaries', receive an 8 per cent payment from the US office for the services it provided the US office from Australia.

A couple of months before, the CFO had called me following a referral from a US client.

Given we have a US–Australia tax specialisation, they called us to see if we would prepare their Australian income tax return for their sole Australian company.

The company in Australia had a 'representative office' function.

Its purpose was to source leads in the Australian market and then refer those leads to the US office to complete the sales process and the forming of the business relationship.

The US company was being very careful that what it did in Australia did not give it a 'taxable presence'.

All reasonably standard stuff they thought!

When I asked how they arrived at the 8 per cent, they mentioned that they had a pricing model in Chicago.

They said that the 'Chicago model' was used globally to justify how 8 per cent was 'payment enough' for sourcing sales in Australia.

I persisted with a few questions, as follows:

Question 1:   Are Australian products sold in the marketplace at the same price as New Zealand?

A: No.

Question 2:   Are the costs of servicing sales in New Zealand the same as the cost of servicing sales in Australia?

A: No.

Question 3:   Have you done a review of what companies in Australia not owned by you might charge you for performing the same service?

A: No.

So, with three questions, I could see that CabinetMaker Inc. was relying on a home country pricing model developed with no understanding of the Australian market.

A fatal mistake to make when you are a new company arriving in Expatland.

I attempted to acquaint them with the realities of doing business away from the US.

They were in Expatland now and they had to adapt to the differences in the market.

Needless to say, when the CFO hit me with the comment, *'I will take it to the Board of Directors and come back to you'*, I heard nothing more from them.

We did not accept the engagement.

The aftermath to the above is that recently a story broke in the Australian media that the company, a subsidiary of a US tech company, was being audited by the Australian Taxation Office.

The media reports noted that their transfer pricing practices were suspect.

The global giant failed to heed the quote at the head of this chapter.

They did not want to unlearn what they thought they knew.

They persisted in trying to apply an overseas model without adapting to their new surroundings. As a result, their business practices were found wanting in Australia and abroad.

The above mistake is reasonably common; that is, companies arriving in Expatland believe they can bring their own way of doing business with them. Nine times out of ten that is incorrect.

When companies arrive in Expatland, it pays to go back to first principles, get proper advice and assume nothing. Adapting to your new surroundings in Expatland is essential.

We understand that business owners and entrepreneurs require specific advice from experienced professional advisers in multiple jurisdictions and that a migration tax plan has to be prepared for a company – just as it does for an individual.

CST Tax Advisors continues to develop and invest in our knowledge and expertise so we can assist our clients set up businesses across the globe.

Let us consider two other forms of arriving in Expatland on an unintended basis below.

Example 1: Unintended arrival

A foreign company establishes a branch in the arrival country.

This occurs when senior directors of a foreign company remain directors of the foreign company and they change their personal tax residence.

As is commonly the case, the directors continue to 'run the foreign company' from their new location. They often do this without realising that they have unwittingly brought the foreign company into the purview of their arrival country.

This triggers tax filing and other reporting obligations.

Example 2: Unintended arrival

Shareholders leave their home country to live abroad, and while they may not be directors of the foreign company, they remain nonetheless individual shareholders.

In this instance, many tax regimes will demand that tax be paid on the earnings of the foreign company as the profit belongs to the shareholders now living in their new country.

This tax exposure would arise by the 'controlled foreign corporation' legislation that many countries have.

Next steps

If one or both of these unintended actions has occurred, then there is a need to value the assets of the company and understand the value of the shares in any foreign company.

Often, the 'starting cost base' of the company assets is relevant, because that is the basis upon which future capital gains are calculated. Most clients miss this step unless properly advised.

Companies that 'arrive' on an unintentional basis now have two tax returns to do.

When we identify where this has occurred, we move quickly to address it.

Planned arrivals

When we have an opportunity to work with clients ahead of their departure, we can plan how best to 'move the company'.

We ensure that as the foreign company may continue to have foreign tax compliance or reporting obligations (for example, a US LLC), we work with the relevant CST partner firm in the jurisdiction to handle ongoing requirements.

Foreign companies with ongoing tax compliance obligations overseas is something we are well able to handle and deal with. Therefore, our clients value CST Tax Advisors and come to our firm for ongoing support and compliance services across borders.

Doing it *The CST Way*

- We help companies when they arrive in Expatland to go back to first principles and ensure they have reviewed their pricing models.

- We understand that business owners require specific advice and a migration plan for them and their business.

- We develop and invest in our knowledge and expertise continually so we can assist our clients across the globe.

- We help our clients avoid triggering 'unintended arrivals' for their companies established in their home country companies.

- We help companies work out the starting point for asset valuations when they arrive in Expatland by identifying local specialists.

- We work with our global partner firms to integrate business tax solutions for companies moving around Expatland.

CHAPTER 14

THE FINANCIAL STATEMENTS

'To state the facts frankly is not to despair the future nor indict the past.' – John F. Kennedy

Sitting in a boardroom in Hollywood not far from the Mann Chinese Theatre, I was admiring the Golden Teapot that sat at the end of the long conference table on a special teapot stand. As I watched the steam waft out from its spout, Carrie, the office assistant to Benedict Cerrone, told me that every day she changed the style and colour of the teapot depending upon the Benedict's horoscope for the day. Only in Hollywood, I thought to myself.

Benedict was waiting, a colourful fashion identity, who was referred to us to see if we could help his company with their Asia Pacific–US tax and accounting. They were highly geared and they wanted to understand what their options were.

After Benedict had the office assistant pour him his first cup of tea, he opened with a rather amazing statement along the line of *'John, I get monthly financials, but I never look at them as they are too complicated for me to understand'*. Benedict went on to say *'I run my business by mostly looking at how much cash we have in the bank!'*

I expressed some dismay to Benedict and then asked for his set of financials for the last two years. Ten minutes later, in walked his CFO, a relative – who gave me a set of accounts that, by and large, was very technical in its description of assets and it was not at all 'user friendly'.

It was immediately apparent that the company had some financial issues. Not only was there too much inventory on its balance sheet as a percentage of total sales, its debt percentage was again much higher than I considered prudent for companies in that industry.

In a footnote, I saw a reference to covenants that the company had given to its bank to secure financing. When I asked Benedict whether he understood what that was, he said that 'financial statements were not his area'!

This was not a small company and, indeed, sales exceeded US$100M.

The above story highlights that many entrepreneurs setting up abroad can succeed for a while, even though they don't understand their financial statements!

This is not what we accept from clients.

We ensure that our clients understand their financial statements.

Let's consider how we put this into practice.

We understand that terminology, such as 'intangible assets', can make appreciating the financial position of a business somewhat inaccessible. Therefore we don't use complicated language in any financial statements we prepare for clients.

For example, 'intangible assets' might alternatively be described in our chart of accounts as 'patents' or 'trademarks'.

As the majority of clients are not accountants, one of our key objectives in the preparation of financial statements is to make the process as straightforward, clear and concise as possible.

This includes how we describe assets and liabilities in plain, everyday language.

We keep this in mind when we ask for data and as we go through the process of preparing financial statements for the business or client.

Our view is that the simpler we can make financial statements for our clients, the easier it will be for them to make decisions.

Who reads our work?

Given our central role is to assist global clients with planning their tax accounting and structuring affairs, we recognise that many third parties will review, assess and then act upon the financial statements or other documents that we prepare.

Therefore, it is not only important for us to determine who will be reading our financial statements and documentation, but also why they will be reading it.

Only then can we ensure that it is presented in a way that it is easy to understand and use. Our goal is to present information in an accurate, user-friendly manner where possible.

The external parties who review our financial statements, tax returns and our letters of advice could include our clients' other family members, their financial planner, solicitor, insurance specialist or their bankers.

In some unfortunate cases, a court or tribunal will read our financial statements, tax returns or advice letters. Hence, we also are respectful of what we say and how we say it.

Therefore, in terms of who reads and or reviews our work, it is a very broad class of people, and as such, it is incumbent upon us to ensure this information is presented professionally and in an accessible way.

Percentage analysis

One of the more useful tools we use when presenting financial statements to our clients is to add percentage analysis to the package.

We show percentage data alongside the numbers.

The reason for this is so that our clients can see how income and expenses levels have changed year on year. Data is central to decision making, so seeing 'numbers only' without the trend line of what has been happening to those numbers over a five-year period does not convey enough information.

As an example, a 30 per cent increase in stock levels, year on year, may point to the fact that obsolete stock is being kept too long and not written off.

The central point is that static data presented as 'accounting regulators' is usually not how our clients want to see the data. For the business clients, we might present a 'business snapshot' document such as the one below.

The business snapshot

On one page, we might present key data over the last five years on the following key items:

	Year 1	Year 2	Year 3	Year 4	Year 5
	$	$	$	$	$
Gross Income					
Operating expenses					
Non-operating expenses					
Cash					
Debtors					
Wages					
Taxes paid					
Profit					
Investments					
Loans					

A simple one-page document showing this high-level data gives our client a trend line from which to probe and ask further questions about their business.

The private client snapshot

In the private client context, we might prepare the 'private client snapshot', as follows:

	Year 1	Year 2	Year 3	Year 4	Year 5
	$	$	$	$	$
Net family wealth					
Net family income					
Total family shares					
Total family cash					
Total family shares					
Total family debt/ Total family wealth					

While this may seem reasonably straightforward, you might be surprised just how few private clients track this data over a five-year time frame.

In our view, without tracking key numbers, it is next to impossible to measure progress.

Doing it *The CST Way*

- One of our key objectives in preparing financial statements is to make sure clients understand them.

- We describe assets and liabilities in plain, everyday language.

- As we know a wide range of people will read our clients' financial statements, we present information in a user-friendly way.

- We utilise percentage analysis for clients seeking to understand trends in their business.

- We help our clients track their key numbers over the last five years so they can pick out problem areas and spot issues.

- We give our clients a simple one-page report that pulls all the key data together for them to interpret.

CHAPTER 15

TRUST MANAGEMENT IN EXPATLAND

'When it comes to Trusts, be clear who you are trusting.' – Nefton Basil

'You can't be serious', I thought (the words of John McEnroe were ringing in my ears). It was 23 February 2007 and Steve, a pilot client of mine, had just explained to me how he had transferred over seven figures to an international investment and trust company that was offering a tax and investment solution based in the Channel Islands. I was in Sydney and just about to cut a birthday cake for my then nine-year-old daughter, Natalie. I was incredulous.

I could not believe that Steve would do that without checking with us first.

Steve assured me that everything was okay. His first officer explained the trust solution to him while they were on a long-haul flight to the UK.

The first officer was a former financial planner who had a contact that would see them when they reached London. Steve was assured that the solution would be tax effective when they returned home to Australia. I asked to see the written advice. There was none.

The sad reality is that in many parts of the world, financial advisers sell investment products via long-term contracts using insurance bonds or closed-end trusts.

Usually these products are not at all effective for tax purposes when our client leaves Expatland.

In this case (to make matter worse), the trustee was owned by the financial adviser's parent company and therefore, was not independent. There was a conflict of interest.

It was the year before the collapse of Lehman. Steve told me how great it was that their money was safe and sound in an insurance company product.

Steve planned to return home the next year and this product would 'roll up' and be tax-free until maturity, which was 25 years from now.

When I asked Steve why he had not come to us for some tax advice, his answer was *'All my other pilot friends are doing this and they have received advice!'*

Not a great answer. However, it was clear to me Steve had failed to think about the *'What can go wrong?'* question. Steve had not thought about how circumstances can change quickly.

Indeed, investment products and trust law is complex enough without being able to unwind a structure and access your capital for 25 years!

The establishment of a trust solution requires a lot of thought and planning.

We make sure our clients understand the four golden rules of setting up a trust:

1. Ensure the bank or financial advisory firm managing your money does not own the trustee company that will be the trustee of your trust. This prevents a conflict of interest.

2. Understand how you can unwind the trust or investment arrangement.

3. Recognise that long-term solutions require tax contingency planning before you sign on the dotted line. As your residency can change, so can you tax position.

4. Make sure you understand if you can access trust income and/or capital to pay taxes that may become due on the gains of the trust.

Before delving into some further issues associated with trust management, I will cover just a few central points about how trusts work for those who may not have worked with trusts.

-   A trust is an arrangement whereby a trustee has a fiduciary obligation to deal with property over which they have control for the benefit of one or more beneficiaries who are able to enforce such an obligation.

-   Beneficiaries may be individuals, corporations, or indeed other trusts (such as a charitable trust).

-   All trusts have a trust deed. At a high level, this is a document that outlines the rules that the trustee must follow in relation to the property they control.

-   Common objectives for utilising trusts are to protect assets and ensure that beneficiaries are able to benefit financially from the trust in a manner that suits the family group and in accordance with the wishes of the settlor of the trust.

• The discretionary trust is the most common trust used by business owners and investors. They are generally set up to hold family and/ or business assets for the benefit of providing asset protection and tax-planning benefits for family members.

The trust deed: Its importance

The trust deed is the most important document of a trust as it establishes and defines terms and conditions upon which the trust must be operated and managed.

More specifically, the trust deed sets out the beneficiaries of the trust, as well as the end date of the trust and the conditions upon which the trustee holds the property for the beneficiaries.

In managing trusts for clients – which we do through CST Trustees Limited – we always ensure we understand the trust deed to assist our client understands all related tax issues and to make certain the beneficiaries know their rights and obligations.

Actions undertaken outside the provisions set out in the trust deed can be deemed by a court of appropriate jurisdiction to be null and void. The implications of an action being null and void can reach further than the act simply being treated as if it did not occur.

An invalid act of a trustee can result in unwanted taxation implications for the trustee, and a breach of the trustee's duties can lead to personal liability for damages or alternatively unwanted consequences for beneficiaries.

The best approach in dealing with trust management and planning is to treat every trust deed as unique and therefore refer to the provisions in the deed prior to taking any action.

How are trusts taxed?

While a trust is regarded as a taxpayer in some countries (e.g. Australia), in other countries this is not the case. In some countries, the beneficiary is taxed on gains accruing in the trust; in others, it is the original settlor who suffers the tax burden.

We are very well qualified to advise our clients on all aspects of tax affecting their family trust.

Other issues

We explain to clients moving to Expatland that trusts are not always the ideal solution for all family asset management objectives.

One aspect of trust management and planning for our clients is the ability to use a trust to ensure that assets are not unwittingly exported into certain tax jurisdictions when our client changes their residency status.

In advising on this aspect of trust management, it is important to understand how a trust determines its residency status.

For example, in Australia, a trust is regarded as a tax resident of Australia if one of the trustees is a tax resident of Australia. However, in other jurisdictions, the concept of central management and control of the trust is used to determine the residency status of the trust.

We work through all the residency aspects likely to impact our clients when establishing a trust or moving around Expatland with an existing trust.

The key point to note is that it can be a useful exercise to transfer assets from an individual to a trust prior to changing residency and heading into

Expatland. However, like most things, this strategy has its pros and cons.

We play a vital role in helping clients consider asset transfers in and out of trusts and whether this helps them meet their tax and financial objectives.

:

Doing it *The CST Way*

We make sure our clients understand the four golden rules of setting up a trust:

1. Ensure the bank or financial advisory firm managing your money does not own the trustee company that will be the trustee of your trust. This prevents conflicts of interest.

2. Understand how you can unwind the trust or investment arrangement.

3. Recognise that long-term solutions require tax contingency planning before you sign on the dotted line. As your residency can change, so can your tax position.

4. Make sure you understand if you can access trust income and or capital to pay taxes that may become due on the gains of the trust.

- We always ensure we understand the trust deed so we can assist our clients with understanding all related tax issues.

- We explain to clients moving to Expatland that trusts are not always the ideal solution for all family asset management objectives.

- We work through all the residency aspects likely to impact our clients when establishing a trust or moving around Expatland with an existing trust.

- We play a vital role in helping clients consider asset transfers in and out of trusts and whether this helps them meet their tax and financial objectives.

CHAPTER 16

TRUSTS HEADING TO EXPATLAND

'Ignorance is bliss.' – Thomas Gray

'As I sat in the oak-panelled boardroom of a client's law firm, high up in the MGM Building in Beverly Hills, Los Angeles, I was musing about LA traffic. I was sure that Bill, an Australian client who had arranged this meeting, would be late. Bill was always late.

The year was 2009 and this was my first experience of an estate-planning meeting at a high-end US law firm.

US law firms, particularly the high-end ones, seem to have this buzz about them from the minute you walk out of the lift. It is almost as if you are walking onto a film set.

This view was confirmed when, just like Harvey Specter from *Suits*, my client's lawyer Harvey junior arrived in a three-piece suit. Immediately, I became apprehensive about a couple of things.

Firstly, Harvey junior was flanked by three people at who-knows-what hourly rates!

Secondly, how would Harvey junior react when we laid out all the trusts our client had in Australia. I knew Harvey junior had acted for Bill for a dozen years or so, but I wondered how much he knew about Bill's Australian assets.

It turned out that Harvey junior knew zero about Bill's Australian assets despite being his lawyer.

As a sign of things to come for me in the US, the next three-and-a-half hours proved just how complicated the US tax system is when it comes to offshore trusts and offshore investment companies.

We were not Bill's accountants in the US.

Bill had recently changed his US Certified Public Accountant firm (CPA firm) and as I was starting to travel in and out of the US, Bill wanted me to attend the meeting.

It turned out that Bill had essentially and unwittingly taken his trusts to Expatland with him.

For some of the trusts, Bill was still the individual trustee.

As these trusts were now being managed in the US, they had a US tax presence.

No US taxes had been filed though because Bill thought that as these were Australian trusts there would be no US issues.

This proved incorrect and expensive to fix. Also, there were disclosure issues that were complied with. The non-disclosure penalties had the potential to be significant.

The lesson learnt was that trusts can move to Expatland just as easily as expats themselves.

Bill was also a beneficiary of a number of trusts that he had nothing to do with other than receive money. As the money was retained in Australia within the trust, Bill thought he had no US tax exposures.

Bill was wrong.

The departing trust is a situation that occurs generally when a trustee changes residence from one country to another.

Residency determination

In the Australian context, where an individual trustee of an Australian trust changes residence, then, often, the trust will also change its residence.

In all cases, we need to make sure that when the trustee changes its residence, the tax consequences are identified.

A departing client will typically need to decide, after our cost benefit analysis, whether it is more beneficial to them and their family for the trust to stay a resident in the particular jurisdiction or for the trust to move with them overseas.

Either way, certain strategies must be implemented to ensure that the desired result is correctly managed for our client.

The main factor in determining how the trust will be treated after our client departs is its residency. In the case of trusts in many other jurisdictions, the residence of the majority of trustees decides the residency of the trust.

Therefore, if an individual is changing their tax residency and they have a family trust, it is *The CST Way* to ensure that we advise our client as to the options relevant to their family trust also.

If the immediate and ongoing tax consequences of keeping the trust in its particular form are not advantageous to our client and their family, we can discuss alternative strategies with our client.

Such strategies may include replacing the trustee of the trust with a company that is domiciled in the jurisdiction to which our client has moved, subject to the laws of that jurisdiction. On other occasions, it may be more appropriate for a replacement trustee to be appointed in a third jurisdiction.

An example of the type of analysis we undertake for clients' benefit is shown below.

Scenario

Mr and Mrs Smith call us to request our advice in relation to their move to Hong Kong. They have complicated affairs and a number of family companies and trusts.

They were told by a financial adviser in Hong Kong that their Australian family trust, the Smith Family Trust, should move its assets to Hong Kong and change the trustee of the trust to a Hong Kong company, because there is no capital gains tax in Hong Kong.

The financial adviser wants them to do this as soon as possible so he can start investing.

This is a typical scenario.

Apart from considering their personal assets and liabilities, we also review the consequences of this move for their family trust as requested.

The structure of that trust is such that it has an Australian company, ABC Pty Ltd, as its trustee. We discover that the Smith Family Trust has cash balances and a share portfolio with large unrealised capital gains.

Therefore, simply appointing a foreign trustee will trigger massive tax exposures for the trust.

We suggest that we retain the Australian trustee, but that we establish a new trust for the family in Hong Kong – so that new investments can be made in Hong Kong without the need to trigger capital gains tax liabilities in Australia.

The purpose of the discussion here is to highlight the fact that planning for a departing trust is very important.

Our approach to this area is to recognise that trusts are long-term family vehicles, and just because a client may move to a new country, it does not mean that they should have to wind up their trust and forgo all the benefits that it has provided them.

Given our international tax and trust knowledge, we will be able to help our client make important decisions such as this.

Doing it *The CST Way*

- We help our clients understand the tax consequences of their trustee changing residence.

- We perform a cost benefit analysis to assist our clients with determining whether their trustee should change residence.

- We make sure our clients recognise that trusts are long-term family vehicles, and just because a client may move to another country, their trust does not need to.

CHAPTER 17

TRUSTS ARRIVING IN EXPATLAND

'Progress is impossible without change, and those who cannot change their minds, cannot change anything.' - George Bernard Shaw

'Ascot Chambers in Sydney has a rather austere entrance. The décor on the floor of the Senior Counsel I was seeing was functional at best. As I waited for learned counsel, I was optimistic that we had cracked the code (in a planning sense) for a client and his family on the move to Australia. The client had a substantial pension trust abroad and we were looking at how it may be protected from Australian tax during the client's period of secondment in Australia.

Our mandate had been to examine how international assets could be held in a foreign pension plan. We had begun planning for our client's arrival some 12 months prior and this was our final meeting with counsel – to confirm our strategy worked.

Some two hours later, we left the Chambers with the good news that our tax-planning strategies, indeed, were rock solid and our client's result was as 'good as gold'.

The particular rules that we worked with for the benefit of our client have since been repealed.

However, the work we did at the time benefited our client for the years they lived in Australia before returning home.

Part of the reason for our success was the time and effort we put into understanding our client's offshore trust and pension structure before he arrived in Australia.

Moving around Expatland while being in control of trusts is complicated and should not be done lightly.

Arriving into Expatland with a trust and no plan was a recipe for disaster.

We studied the trust deed, considered the material terms, and examined what changes could be made to the trust deed prior to our client becoming an Australian resident.

Conferring with our client and his international advisers, we were able to explain what changes we wanted and the reasons why.

That client's fact pattern and global family were part of the solution implemented, but the key point was that early planning was the reason for getting it right.

Arriving with a trust

Where a new individual client has changed their residence and they are the trustee of a foreign trust, it is clear that this trust is also likely to become a resident of the arrival country.

In other cases, even if the client ceases being the trustee in specific jurisdictions such as Australia, tax income on pre-migration transfers assets to foreign trusts. The Australian 'anti-tax avoidance' rules are formidable, but they are by no means out of the ordinary.

Many other tax systems tax transfers set up to avoid arrival country taxation.

When clients appoint us as tax advisers and accountants for their trusts, we conduct a detailed study of the fact pattern to understand how those assets came to be owned by the trust. We need this information to know whether these pre-arrival transfers into trusts are likely to be that effective in the arrival country.

Furthermore, as part of the new client on-boarding process, we always review the trust deed and, where appropriate, we have it legally reviewed to ensure that it is validly constituted. It may be that terms of law in overseas jurisdictions have no application in the arrival country and that definitions may need modification.

Other concepts, which might be recognised abroad, such as 'community title', might be used in the trust deed, but these concepts might have no application in the arrival country.

Once this is done, we are then in a position to understand how the trust operates and have the previous set of financial statements reviewed.

While these financial statements would likely have been prepared by a foreign firm of accountants, a review of these financial statements is essential to give us an appreciation of the issues we are likely to face when the time comes to do the tax return.

The arriving trust may still have reporting obligations in the country in which it was established. If this is the case, we ensure that we work cooperatively with the foreign accounting firm acting for the trust and the client.

It may also be the case that there are foreign protectors (referred to as 'appointors' in Australia) or other people who have an ongoing role in the management of the trust.

If so, we may need to provide information to these people to address the management and ongoing operational issues around the trust. The arriving trust may also have foreign debt obligations, so we should ensure that the deed has an appropriate indemnity clause.

As the accountants for arriving trusts, we would prepare an initial set of financial statements to reflect the position as at the date of arrival into Expatland. This is particularly important if the arriving trust has a business or significant assets.

Often, the cost base of trust assets must be understood on the day the trust first enters Expatland.Usually this will be the market value of the assets on the day of the trust's arrival, but not always.

Doing it *The CST Way*

- When clients appoint us as tax advisers and accountants for their trusts, we conduct a detailed study of the fact pattern to understand how those assets came to be owned by the trust.

- We always review the trust deed, and where appropriate, we will have it legally reviewed to ensure it is validly constituted.

- We ensure that if the 'arriving trust' still has reporting obligations in its formation country, we work cooperatively with the foreign accounting firm acting for the trust and the client.

- We would prepare an initial set of financial statements for all 'arriving trusts' to reflect the value of assets on the day of the arrival of the trust in Expatland.

CHAPTER 18

PENSION FUND PLANNING ISSUES

'Chase your passion, not your pension.' – Denis Waitley

'While the above may be true, there is also no point throwing your pension away. That was exactly what my client, Peter, was about to do unless he delayed his plans to move to the US with his wife, Helen, for a few months..

Peter had built up a sizeable pension fund balance in Australia. It was the product of 30 years working in the film and entertainment business. Over the previous ten years, Peter had been a senior executive working for a chain of movie theatres in Singapore.

As such, international tax had not crossed his mind much. Peter and Helen had grandchildren living in Santa Monica. They were keen to retire and enjoy the good life in a new location.

Expatland beckoned.

Peter had calculated that he would be able to fund his future Santa Monica lifestyle through a combination of personal savings and by accessing his Australian pension. Everything was set.

Pension payments in Australia were tax free, so Peter thought that Uncle Sam would also not tax them.

Unfortunately, that was not the case. In the US, such income streams are taxable if you are a US tax resident.

We stopped Peter sending his pension to the US in the nick of time.

We collapsed Peter's Australian pension and enabled Peter to take his capital to the US and invest it in the US tax efficiently.

Disaster averted.

This case study highlights why, in order to enjoy your pension, you must consider the impact of foreign tax laws when you are changing jurisdiction.

In delivering service to clients *The CST Way*, we consider the impact of any overseas move on their home country pension.

The underlying motivation for establishing a pension fund is typically based on a desire to save funds for retirement so that there is no reliance on government pensions. Thus, it means that having the maximum amount available in the pension plan that is not eroded by taxation, is a primary objective.

It is folly to think that a tax-advantaged regime in one country with respect to pension funds will axiomatically apply in Expatland. That is rarely the case.

We have extensive knowledge of the taxation issues relevant to pensions and superannuation. This enables us to assist clients with compliance and planning in relation to this important area of their lives.

When expats leave their home country for Expatland, there are many aspects of tax that need to be considered prior to departure and pension fund planning is often a priority.

We can also help clients understand whether moving their pension fund to their arrival country is a practical option. For those expats that have their pension fund in the UK, it may actually be worthwhile moving their pension with them. There are particular rules to address this.

A Qualifying Recognised Overseas Pension Scheme (QROPS) is an overseas pension scheme that meets certain requirements set by Her Majesty's Revenue and Customs (HMRC). A QROPS can receive transfers of UK pension benefits without incurring an unauthorised payment and scheme sanction charge.

In Australia, for example, pension funds are only considered to be complying under the governing legislation if they remain within the Australian tax jurisdiction. This means, that the trustee must remain an Australian resident.

Therefore, in the case of an expat, relocation can inadvertently trigger a tax liability. Steps need to be taken prior to departure.

The key point is that as we are close to our clients and actively involved in their financial and tax affairs, we are well placed to assist them in this area.

Arriving in Expatland

Similarly, many expats arrive in Expatland with their home country pension fund in place. Therefore, they must adhere to the rules in their home country and their arrival country in relation to this pension fund.

One of the specialist skills we possess as part of *The CST Way* is in advising clients how foreign pension plans will be treated as they move around the globe. We can advise clients on QROPS and other similar regimes.

Doing it *The CST Way*

• We help clients consider the impact of moving around on their pension fund.

• We have extensive knowledge of the taxation issues relevant to pensions and superannuation. This enables us to assist clients with compliance and planning in relation to this important area of their lives.

• We can help clients understand whether moving their pension fund to their arrival country is a practical option.

• We remain close to our clients through the continual review of the R-Factor Question® so we are well placed to assist them with managing their pension planning needs.

CHAPTER 19

DEATH AND TAXES: WHAT WE NEED TO KNOW

'In this world, nothing can be said to be certain, except death and taxes.' – Benjamin Franklin

''Forty per cent of how much?', said Bob, my new client, as I gave him the news that the country home he had just bought, not too far from Stonehenge, would be subject to UK inheritance tax! Bob and I were meeting for a 'first-up' at his new holiday home and the topic of UK inheritance came up. It came as quite a shock to him to realise that 40 per cent of the value of his home could find its way to the Chancellor of the Exchequer.

Bob, a recent arrival from New Zealand, had worked with a couple of previous accountants before us, but he had not been advised about inheritance tax.

He was unaware that he could have avoided this potential liability had he undertaken some proper structuring and tax planning.

When clients move to Expatland, we conduct a detailed review of the estate-planning laws of that country to ensure they are informed about the impact of death and taxes.

Some countries view death as constituting a disposal of your assets for tax purposes, while others do not.

Working with CST Tax Advisors is a sure-fire way of ensuring you have strategies in place to address this final impost on your assets.

As part of our approach to advising our clients in relation to estate planning, we work with them and their appointed attorneys to plan for the impact of their untimely death.
We focus on the importance of their having a well-structured, flexible Will.

A poorly-structured Will can result in assets passing to individuals whom our clients do not wish to benefit under the Will.

Usually this unpleasant prospect motivates most people to give the matter serious attention.

In general terms, an estate plan is a document that considers:

- what assets go to whom

- if there are young children, who are guardians of those children?

- who is to be the executor of the estate?

- who would make the decisions as to the education, maintenance and benefits for any young children surviving their parents?

- what specific bequests should be made?

- if an estate is to continue for a number of years, how it is to be managed and maintained as per tax and accounting obligations?

- what insurances are necessary to cover death duties?

In Australia, for example, a properly structured testamentary trust allows the children to benefit from income in an estate – long before they get access to the majority of the capital.

A tax-efficient Will can ensure that these children do not suffer the burden of higher taxation.

We often speak with parents that do not wish their children to simply receive the full value of the estate in a lump sum, even at 18 years of age.

Some parents believe that the children may not be mature enough to deal with the management of the estate or the burden of wealth.

Our role

We make sure that where a testamentary trust is formed, we discuss with our client whether the surviving spouse might wish to be supported by one or two other people to assist in the role of executor.

In times of distress, we understand that it is often beneficial for the surviving partner to be supported in the administration of the estate and the decision making by having one or two people the family trusts as co-executors.

We also assist clients plan for guardianship issues in cases where there are young children involved.

Part of the planning process is ensuring that we are working with an insurance specialist to give our clients the opportunity to have a sufficient level of insurances in place. We also consider if the estate plan has enough capital to fund the life of the non-working spouse and their family, as well as making sure there are enough funds so that all debts can be paid off.

Our role as our client's tax advisers and accountants often results in us being asked to prepare a cash flow forecast for them and to work with the financial planner to understand the impact of taxation on future income available to beneficiaries of the estate.

Implications for expats and their estate plans

When clients become expats, there are added complications in relation to dealing with death and taxes. There is always the unfortunate possibility for the expat that death may occur while they are away from their home country (which may mean they are away from the extended family).

The risk of not having a properly structured Will while living in a foreign country is significant.

In our experience, it is very important that our clients to understand the full ramifications of passing away and how their Will, if there is one, would be recognised in Expatland. The following points are some of the high-level issues.

- We consider whether a local Will is needed in Expatland.

- In the case of an expat client with young children, a key issue is whether the young children would be allowed to leave the foreign country in the unfortunate case of the death of both parents. It may be that a document should be filed with a solicitor showing clear authorisation for grandparents or other relations to be able to make decisions concerning the children. These documents may need to be stamped and/or filed with the guardian office in the foreign country.

- Also in the above case, the proposed guardian may live in another country. That presents issues in terms of which country the children need to move to so they can live with the guardians.

- Work needs to be undertaken to recognise that the laws of Expatland may require those children to do national service. This may actually prevent them from leaving their arrival country.

- It is also the case that an executor in one country may find it very difficult to administer the estate if the bulk of the assets are held in a different country. It is important to make sure that one executor, professional or otherwise, resides in the country where the deceased lived and worked. This co-executor will be able to assist in the process of managing the divestment of property under the Will.

- Bereaved family members may need assistance from these professionals to help manage the sale of assets, the repayment of debt and the collection of monies from government departments.

Overall, the key objectives of a good estate plan are to:

- identify the assets owned by the deceased

- where there are likely to be young children, consider how custody of those assets should be passed to a testamentary trust that arises upon death of either parent

- consider what is to happen with income earned in relation to the testamentary trust

- if no trust is to be created on death, there should be clarity regarding who gets what assets and in what proportions

- a list of important contacts (including the financial planner, insurance and risk specialist and executor) should be evident in the estate plan and this would be kept up to date

- the executor should be made aware that they are an executor and be willing and able to act in the role

- guardians should be made aware that they are guardians, and be willing and able to act in the role.

Multiple copies of the Will should exist and be kept in at least two locations, with the accountant and the lawyer. The Will should be reviewed on a regular basis.

Our approach in the delivery of *The CST Way* calls for consideration of a variety of different strategies.

Doing it *The CST Way*

- Working to ensure clients have strategies in place to address estate taxes.

- We focus on the importance of having a well-structured flexible Will.

- We often help parents plan testamentary trust formation so they do not have to leave large amounts to young children before they are mature enough to handle the capital sums.

- We also consider the guardianship issues that should be addressed in cases where estates are likely to have young children.

- We also consider if the estate plan has enough capital to fund the life of the surviving spouse and children.

CHAPTER 20

PLANNING FOR THE YEAR END: THINGS TO DO

'Productivity is never an accident. It is always the result of a commitment to excellence, intelligent planning, and focused effort.' - Paul J Meyer

'It's time for me to get home' Marty said to me as he and I were sitting in a corporate box at the Hong Kong Sevens. He and I had just watched Australia win its first game over Western Samoa. It was March 2011.

I had known Marty for many years. Given his significant spread of global assets and his complex employee share plan position with an investment bank, I knew there would be a lot to plan and get done prior to the impending 30 June year-end deadline.

Marty told me that he had agreed with the bank that he would leave the bank on 31 May and take up employment with them in Sydney on 1 July.

While all of that sounded fine, there were a few complicating factors. One of the major issues was that he would be moving off the Hong Kong payroll and onto the Australian payroll. As such, there was likely to be a termination payment paid sometime after 30 June. This would involve not only payments in respect of his employee shares, but also long service leave and annual leave as well as a 'golden handcuff' to make sure he did not leave the Australian business anytime soon!

The significance of all of this was that some of these payments had the potential to be taxed in Australia, notwithstanding that some of them were earned while Marty was employed overseas.

In view of the looming year end, we had to work fast.

We negotiated with Marty's employer to have many of these payments paid to him while he was a resident of Hong Kong and before the year end in Australia.

Had we waited until Marty returned as many accountants do (often through lack of communication or knowledge of their client's movements), then it would have been too late to save Marty any significant amount of income tax.

It is, therefore, commonly the case that when employees move around the globe and/or return home, a lot of year-end planning needs to be done to make sure that tax is not paid on income earned abroad.

Marty's story is not unusual, unfortunately, based on my experience.

The key then with year-end planning for global private clients is to understand the multiple year ends that may apply to their different global income streams and then to be alert to what action steps might mitigate unplanned tax impacts.

We spend a lot of time helping clients prepare their tax-planning options well before the end of the year is upon them.

We use this planning period to look at their business and consider their tax-planning options.

A key function in our role as tax advisers and chartered accountants is to help our clients understand what their impending tax obligation for the current financial year is likely to be.

We believe that as a matter of good order, our clients should be on top of their financial position throughout the year and it is our role to assist them with identifying tax-planning issues that they may have overlooked.

Our ability to accurately forecast the year-end position for our clients allows them to properly plan their tax payment cash flows over the next 12 months.

To assist them with planning their tax payments over a 12-month period, we provide them with a special report called a Tax Cashflow Management Report.

Tax Management Cash Flow Report

The Tax Management Cash Flow Report is prepared as part of our year-end planning efforts. It conveys information to our client as to when the relevant year's income tax is likely to be due and payable.

Our clients are highly appreciative of this service as it helps them stay on top of various payment dates throughout the year.

In fact, many clients report that before coming to CST Tax Advisors, their previous accountants would ring them the day before the tax payment date to tell them a tax payment was due.

This is not *The CST Way.*

We believe that only when our business clients understand their future tax payments can they make meaningful decisions about further investments or capital expenditure in their business.

As time progresses, the answer to the *R-Factor Question®* (as discussed earlier in Chapter 1) will change. It is imperative that we understand the current position of our client so that we can factor this in during our planning efforts.

Our view is that a client should have their interim work completed with sufficient time to allow for any tax management steps to be completed well before the year ends.

Part of our year-end planning process is designed to achieve the following three objectives:

1. Clarification as to whether this year is going to result in more tax due than the prior year.

2. Consideration of whether our client has paid sufficient tax throughout the year or whether they will have to pay additional tax in respect of income earned.

3. Consideration as to whether there are any steps that we can assist our client to undertake between now and year end to provide our client with greater saving opportunities.

In preparing our year-end tax plans for our client, we always devote time to consider whether they have generated new sources of passive, employment or business income.

Our year-end planning meeting also allows us to know what plans our client may have for the next 12–24 months.

Generally, our business clients give us key information within three months of the end of the tax year. This then gives us enough time to understand and plan where the taxable income is.

Doing it *The CST Way*

• We spend a lot of time helping clients prepare their tax-planning options.

• We use the planning period to look at clients' business income and consider options that have clear and relevant application to our clients' specific position.

• We believe that as a matter of good order, our clients should be on top of their financial position throughout the year, and it is our role to assist them with identifying tax-planning opportunities well before year end.

• We are able to forecast the year-end position for our clients, which allows them to properly plan their tax payments.

• We prepare specialised reports, including the Tax Management Cash Flow Report.

CHAPTER 21

COMMUNICATION 101: HOW WE TALK WITH OUR CLIENTS

'The single biggest problem in communication is the illusion that it has taken place.' – George Bernard Shaw

'The headline across the front page of The Australian Financial Review (AFR) was in big, bold typeface. Our client, Luke, a CEO of a well-known listed entertainment company had just been fired by the Board of Directors late the previous day. It was March 2006.

The article began with words '(Luke and company) had agreed that 'in the best interests of the company and its shareholders, Luke would leave the company by 31 March'. This was in seven days.

An interim CEO had been appointed. It was big news.

As I skimmed the article with contained a brief history of Luke, his corporate career and the market analysts' explanation for why he was sacked, my mind was racing ahead to the practicalities of the matter.

Some issues came to mind:

- Had he agreed to all aspects of his termination deal?

- What would be done in regards to his equity compensation plans that still had three years to run?

- What would happen with his company pension plan given it was a specialised type of plan?

- What room was there to negotiate the manner in which we could structure his termination payment?

We did not have much time to work this out. Seven days goes by quickly.

My view about communication is that it has to be timely, direct and get to the heart of the matter.

This is *The CST Way*.

I called Luke on his cell mobile phone, as I knew I needed to get on a plane and get down to Melbourne, where Luke lived.

The call went something like this:

John: *Hi Luke. How are you?*

Luke: *You heard the news?*

John: *Yep, saw it in the AFR this morning. How are you and Kate? I would like to come down and chat through details and options.*

Luke: *Thanks John. That would be great. We have lots to cover. They are not being very accommodating.*

Three hours later, I was driving through the leafy suburb of Toorak, Melbourne, where Luke lived. The business reporters were still outside his home waiting for comments from him.

As I went inside, our work was about to begin.

For the rest of the day, Luke and I looked at the compensation being offered as part of the termination deal. We thought about all the tax issues in relation to the termination and how we would like to have things structured. There were a few issues, however, related to employment law, which I could not solve. I knew that I would have to extend my stay until the next day.

One issue was how the company was going to measure a performance award for Luke. I called an employment law partner I knew at a Melbourne firm for his thoughts. By the evening, we had some ideas about how we wanted to structure the separation deal.

The following morning, Luke and I met Michael Elkan, a partner at the firm. We spent the next few hours working through some options.

At noon, we delivered our letter in person to the company's head office on Collins Street, Melbourne. We then headed to lunch at the Sofitel on Collins Street. We knew we held an advantage given the politics of the situation.

The company would not want to be involved in a contentious litigation and have Luke in the press over his departure compensation. The sooner they could announce they had reached a settlement over his unexpected departure, the better for everyone.

Luke knew all key players involved in the company, himself having hired the CFO, the Head of Human Resources and indeed the interim CEO.

At 5pm that afternoon, the company called Luke agreeing to all our requests. By giving them a list of options virtually the day after they sacked Luke, our communication was timely, direct and relevant.

This is Communication 101.

Furthermore, by bringing in a respected law firm to present what we wanted for Luke, the public company knew we were ready for action. We also ensured that we were not overreaching in our demands and we played it straight down the line.

We work out what is the best communication style to use with and/or for our clients and we use it.

In the above case, the best communication was face to face. Bringing in the law and making them write the letter overnight was another form of communication.

As clients are different, the manner in which information must be conveyed also needs to be different.

One form of communication is an 'across-the-table' approach of speaking 'to' a client.

Our style is an 'around-the-table' approach. This approach is collaborative and personal.

We find that the 'around-the-table' approach is much more conducive to speaking collaboratively and meeting our client's needs than a lecturing 'across-the-table' approach.

We never sell to our clients.

Our firm's remuneration is not transaction driven. The delivery of services does not require us to 'make the sale'.

Our sole objective is to deliver our technical tax planning, tax compliance and accounting services in line with our *Guiding Philosophy* as outlined in Chapter 1.

Here are some further examples of the 'talking with' clients approach in action in order of preference:

- in person
- on Skype
- on the phone
- email.

While everybody loves email, this does not form our preferred mode of communication when it comes to 'talking with' clients about something important or sensitive. It is, of course, very difficult to convey the right tone in certain issues to clients via email. Clients will always appreciate the personal touch and will usually react positively to the effort we make.

Important or sensitive topics are best done in person.

We are in the 'people business' and while some say that 'shaking hands and pressing the flesh' is an outmoded form of communication, our view is that a face-to-face meeting is still the best way to communicate information.

We learn much more from our new clients through the face-to-face 'first-ups' than we could by any other medium. Many clients give us feedback that their previous accountants did everything by phone or email and, as such, there was a sense of being disconnected.

Client's coming to us from Big 4 firms often say that they felt like they were being 'processed' or just like a 'small a cog in a big wheel'.

Given my history of having founded the firm with only a handful of early clients in 1992, I can assure you not one of those early clients ever felt like 'a cog in a wheel'.

This approach holds just as true today. Our clients are the reason the doors stay open and we value that highly.

The importance of communicating face to face cannot be overstated.

Skype is better than the phone.

How we deliver a message can be as important as the technical message we convey.

Communication should be prompt; more so when the news is bad.

If 'unpleasant news' needs to be communicated, such as a missed payment deadline or an impending tax lodgement deadline, our view is that communicating with our client should be done immediately via the phone, not email.

There is a natural tendency to deliver good news quickly and unpleasant news slowly!

That, however, is not *The CST Way.*

Generally, bad news needs to be delivered at greater speed than good news so the problem can be dealt with.

Anyone can deliver good news. Delivering bad news takes empathy and honesty.

Our clients always appreciate prompt communication as well as a suggested course of action to address any issue that might have arisen.

Clients first and foremost.

In terms of how we talk with our clients, we do not blur the line between adviser and friend.

We certainly highly value our relationships with our clients and respect the warmth in them, but we cannot communicate as friends.

However, our philosophy is that our relationships are 'client relationships first and foremost'.

To work on the basis of a friendship can introduce problems and blur the lines.

We avoid that. We need to, so that we can deliver on our *Guiding Philosophy*.

Our professional burden and obligation contained therein supersedes any friendship-related obligations.

Why we talk with our clients: C.A.R.E.

We are reasonably prescriptive when it comes to *'Communication 101: How we talk with our clients'*, because it is fundamental to demonstrating **C.A.R.E.**

Failure to show C.A.R.E. is why clients generally leave accounting practices feeling unappreciated. It is rarely about other things like fees.

C.A.R.E. goes to the heart of our empathy objective.

We believe there is no point being the smartest people in the room if we do not show our clients that we C.A.R.E.

C.A.R.E. is always the basis of a successful professional relationship, just as care is the basis of a personal relationship. As an example, a random email sent the day before a filing deadline is due does not demonstrate C.A.R.E. It is careless and shows poor planning on behalf of the professional in question.

That is not *The CST Way.*

C.A.R.E stands for the following:

Clarity – our communication is clear and not overly technical. We ensure that we communicate the message in a way that our client understands.

Attention – we pay attention to what our clients want and we always show them that their needs and requirements are important.

Responsiveness – when we, as professional client advisers, become aware that a client opportunity or need has arisen, we respond. If the matter is complex, then our professionals will work with their partner to attend to our client's needs.

Energy – if we have follow-up action to do, we display energy and a sense of urgency to our client. Our business requires energy and commitment. If we do not have it, our clients can see it.

Therefore showing C.A.R.E. is why I believe *Communication 101: How we talk with our clients* is the most important topic in *The CST Way*.

What we communicate to clients

The information we communicate to clients is always based on a detailed consideration of their current personal, family and financial position.

General questions in relation to tax return documents can be asked via email or phone, but advice-orientated work should ideally always involve face-to-face meetings.

Face-to-face meetings (Skype or otherwise) allow a more detailed discussion of the subject in real time to draw out issues and points of view that simply cannot be addressed via email.

Management of client expectations

A common theme with other accounting firms holds true to the stereotypical view of communication, which is that accountants only speak to clients at tax time.

This is not *The CST Way.*

We have a model that explains how we like to work with clients *throughout* the year, which illustrates our collaborative approach. It is represented in the advisory cycle below.

The advisory cycle

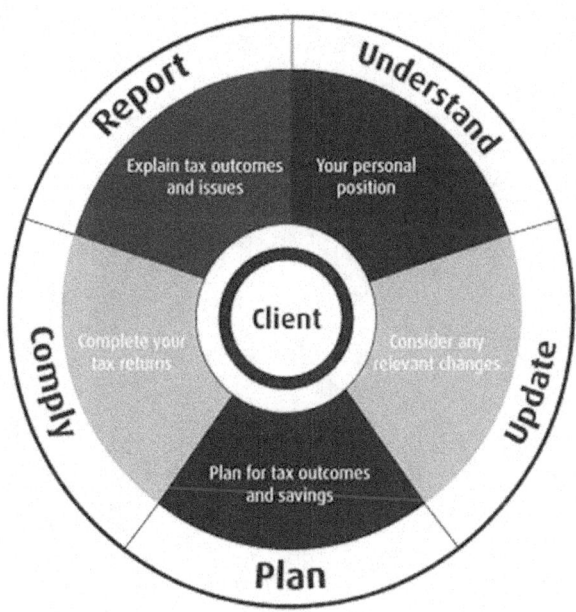

The first step is to understand our client's position.

The next is to ensure we stay updated with changes in our client's position.

During the year, we like to plan for tax outcomes and savings for our clients. At year end (or throughout the year), we help our clients comply with their income tax requirements and the process is completed as we report to our client and explain all outcomes and issues to them.

The advisory cycle then repeats as we move forward during the year.

Doing it *The CST Way*

- We work out what is the best communication style to use with and/or for our particular client, and we use it.

- Our form of communicating with our client is an 'around-the-table' approach. It is a collaborative and personal style of working together.

- We never sell to our clients. We advise them.

- Our view is that a face-to-face meeting is the best way to communicate rather than email or phone.

- We know our clients are the reason our doors stay open and this comes through in the way we communicate with empathy.

- We understand that bad news needs to be delivered more quickly than good news because often actions have to be taken to fix something.

- We do not blur the line between advisor and friend.

- Our philosophy is client first and foremost.

- We show C.A.R.E. when we communicate.

- C.A.R.E. stands for Clarity, Attention, Responsiveness, and Energy.

- The information we communicate to clients is always based on a detailed consideration of their current personal, family and financial position.

CHAPTER 22

TIME FOR A CHAT?

**'A small fire left alone soon becomes a big one.' -
Annie Sookias**

*It was 2009 and I had not spoken with Michael for about
18 months. You can imagine my surprise when I got a
letter from a liquidator asking me if I had any money
due from Michael as Michael's company had gone into
liquidation!*

This was news to me as I was Michael's accountant.
I took the news with a mix of astonishment and guilt

As most accountants reading this will relate, the
pace of my professional practice had meant that I

had put off calling Michael more than a few times as I had 'other things' to focus on.

How could Michael's company have hit financial troubles so quickly and why did he not reach out?

Michael was in the convention business. He had successfully established himself in Australia and in late 2007 he launched his business in Asia by founding a business in Hong Kong. His market research had told him that Hong Kong was at the beginning of a growth phase when it came to organising conventions for the trade industry, building and construction industry.

A little older than me at the time, it turned out that Michael had expanded too rapidly, borrowed some money to put on a major exhibition in the hope that he could sell convention space by attracting people to display their products at his exhibition.

When the financial crisis hit in 2008 the discretionary spending that many companies used to make on sending delegates to conventions stopped overnight. The downturn severely affected Michael's Asian business.

As Michael had borrowed in Australia and given personal guarantees for these loans, he was exposed.

While both his Australian and Hong Kong company was on the way down, his personal life was also unravelling. His wife left him and his personal credit dried up.

It was the perfect storm.

As it happened, Michael did owe us some outstanding fees, but as I looked at the liquidator's letter it occurred to me – I had let him down.

When I spoke to Michael after the collapse of the company, he admitted to me that he thought about ringing me, but my previous words of advice were on his mind.

That advice had been not to expand too quickly. I suggested that he pre-sell advertising or bring in partners to co-host major trade shows in Hong Kong.

Michael, though the eternal optimist, took on the sole risk of hiring a major convention centre and after the 2008 crisis no one was in the mood to spend up at the time.

I had not allowed *'Time for a chat'*.

That was the last time I allowed that to happen.

After that, I put in place a system that has allowed me to monitor communication with my clients.

At CST Tax Advisors, we all believe strongly in *'Time for a chat'*.

Part of maintaining a client relationship is sometimes recognising the need to chat to a client before they do.

Our approach now is that each principal makes it their job to regularly monitor the frequency of communication they have with their clients within their portfolio.

For example, each month for a given level of clients, each of our principals lists those clients that need to be contacted that month and in relation to which key issues. These calls are then scheduled for either the first or second half of the month.

Time for a chat is our philosophy of speaking with clients regularly just to check in and work through changes that may have occurred over the preceding 12 months and changes that our client may have in mind over the following 12 months.

At the very least, the Fact Finder needs to be updated by reviewing it with our client once a year.

On many occasions, the 'Time for a chat' philosophy uncovers new issues or concerns that our client may have.

Whenever an idea or a strategy occurs to us as part of the annual or semi-annual review, or otherwise, we believe it is time for a chat.

Earlier in Chapter 1, we discussed in depth the *R-Factor Question®*. Making time for a chat is a good forum to raise new strategies and things that can benefit our clients.

We generally maintain a client's planning agenda as this arises out of the *R-Factor Question®* work we have been doing with them.

If this is updated on an annual basis, with client objectives noted, then applying the principles noted in the *R-Factor Question®* provides us with a very good idea of how we can work to improve our client's affairs.

The philosophy of *'Time for a chat'* means that we also try to schedule an annual meeting with our client and their financial adviser. Given that we have a very good understanding of the tax, accounting and business issues affecting our client, our presence at this meeting is essential and usually helps enhance the outcome of the meeting.

How we interact with our clients in *The CST Way* is to keep a continual eye on the two documents – the Fact Finder and the *R-Factor Question®* – and combine these with the *What Can Go Wrong Question?*, so we can hold a thorough planning meeting with each client at least annually.

We also plan an annual agenda with the team of complementary professionals working with our client, including their lawyer, their financial adviser and their insurance agent, as the case may be.

The value we create for our clients through this process is very rewarding.

Our view is that *'Time for a chat'* is a key part of our philosophy and it ensures that we can always assist our clients in a proactive manner. This has a very positive impact on the professional relationship overall.

Our experience with new clients is that by using the *'Time for a chat'* approach, they quickly move from saying *'I have done this …'* to *'I am considering doing this; what do you think?'*

Most of the clients that come to CST Tax Advisors from other firms generally have the habit of telling their advisers after the fact that something has been done. We like to instil a *'before-the-fact approach'*. *Time for a chat* does that. When this is in operation with clients, we know we have achieved the desired professional/client working relationship.

.

Doing it *The CST Way*

- We strongly believe in 'Time for a chat'.

- We know that part of maintaining a client relationship is sometimes recognising the need to chat before the client does.

- We make it the principal's job to regularly monitor the frequency of communication they have with clients in their portfolio and routinely check in.

- We perform 'Time for a chat' at least annually and we make a point of also updating the Fact Finder during this chat.

- We find that on many occasions, 'Time for a chat' uncovers new issues or concerns that our clients have.

- We generally maintain a client's planning agenda, as this arises out of the R-Factor Question® work we are doing with them.

- We also work on the annual agenda with the team of complementary professionals working with our clients during the 'Time for a chat' process.

- We like to instil a before-the-fact approach, and 'Time for a chat' does this.

CHAPTER 23

OUR PEOPLE

'We must open the doors of opportunity. But we must also equip our people to walk through those doors.' - Lyndon B Johnson

Vicky Hoffman was my first employee. It was March 1993 and my practice was growing strongly. I had never employed anyone before. It was a new experience employing an accountant to do what I used to do. I was also somewhat unsure if I could afford to pay Vicky!

But I took comfort in the fact that my mentor at the time, Joe Bongiorno, told me that the pathway to business growth was through employing people. Joe put it something like this, *'John, once you employ people, you will be motivated to work out how to pay for them and you will grow your business!'*

I am deeply indebted to Joe for that advice. Joe's brother Tony explained this theory in the following way.

Tony told me the story of the divers who dive off the cliff at Acapulco. He asked me if I knew when they dived. I did not. He said *'John, have a look at them on TV'*. This was way before the internet.

Continuing, Tony said, *'They dive when they see the rocks below them because they know that by the time they get down there, the tide will have brought the water back in. If they dive when they see the water over the rocks, well that will be the end of them, because the tide will have taken the water out and they will be diving onto the rocks!'*

Tony's point was that I had to take the leap of faith and employ people even though it might look like there were rocks below me.

Somewhat of a risk perhaps – but I did it anyway.

I found that the extra time I now had did in fact allow me to keep Vicky Hoffman very busy.

Vicky also taught me an important lesson – that was: to keep your team engaged and challenged, you have to find ways that provide opportunities for them to grow and develop personally and professionally.

Vicky was only four years younger than me when I employed her. I asked her what made her come and work for me, a sole practitioner.

Her answer was insightful.

Vicky said, *'You are a sole practitioner – so I know you will give me an opportunity to do more work and have greater responsibility than I would get at a larger firm. I will work more closely with you and learn more.'*

The light bulb went on. During the following 26 years, I have employed many more people.

Working out what employees want and asking them the *R-Factor Question*® also ensures that I know how our business can help them.

I believe my relationship with our people is like a 'see-saw'. It has to be in balance perfectly or one of us will not be 'happy' with the status quo.

My approach has always been to see our people progress. If they come to a point where they find a better opportunity elsewhere, I am 100 per cent okay with that.

I appreciate their service and the time we had working together.

Lyndon Johnson the architect of the following quote is 100 per cent on point: *'We must open the doors of opportunity. But we must also equip our people to walk through those doors'*.

This is *The CST Way*.

Pick the right people, pay them well, and keep giving them opportunities to grow and develop and move forward, even if moving forward means moving on.

Professional development is one of the most important aspects of building our business and maintaining quality in our service delivery.

We know that it is essential that our professionals are motivated to learn, develop and grow.

We believe that 'learning should be fun' and that this also applies to professional development.

Our goal is to ensure that we foster an environment of learning among all our team members, not only our professional accountants.

Part of developing a professional person is the formal appraisal process.

At the heart of the review process is *'Get it, want it and capacity to do it'* (GWC), a concept developed by Gino Wickman – architect of the great book, *Traction*®.

As noted earlier, *Traction*® describes Gino's EOS in detail and we are very happy to be working with it.

The people that have GWC stay with us at CST; those that do not move on.

Doing it *The CST Way*

- We believe that our relationship with our people is like a 'see-saw'. It has to be in balance perfectly or one of us will not be 'happy' with the status quo.

- We believe that our people must progress personally and professionally.

- Professional development is one of the most important aspects of building our business and maintaining the quality of our service delivery.

- We know and appreciate that it is essential our professionals are motivated to learn, develop and grow.

- We believe that learning should be fun and that this also applies to professional development.

- We foster an environment of learning among all our team members.

- We believe in 'GWC' – that is, our people must all 'get it, want it' and have the 'capacity to do it'.

CHAPTER 24

KNOW YOUR CLIENT: A BRAVE NEW WORLD

'If you can control information, you can control people.' – Tom Clancy

On 16 July 2013, Frank, a longstanding client of our Singapore practice, rang me somewhat alarmed. He said, 'John, please can you help me out as I need to do business and XYZ bank in Singapore has just frozen my account. They won't release my money to me'.

Now I knew that banks in Singapore were becoming a lot more circumspect about opening accounts for new clients. Indeed, in the 'brave new world' that is global banking, the introduction of a number of legislative measures has made it very much more difficult and time consuming to open new bank accounts.

I was, however, surprised to hear that the bank had frozen Frank's bank account. Frank ran a software company in Singapore and it was profitable and highly successful; so much so, that he had recently expanded to the US.

I asked Frank why he thought this might have happened and he mentioned to me that they had introduced some new investors into the company.

Alarm bells went off in my mind.

I asked Frank if he had notified the bank of the change in the shareholders of his company. He said that he had sent new forms in the previous month and his banker had told him all was okay.

In fact, all was not okay.

I rang the bank and discovered that the bank had independently conducted its own company searches. When it discovered that 20 per cent of the shares of the company was now held by US companies, it became concerned because it had no information on the new beneficial owners, including their passports, their residential address details or, indeed, any information of substance.

We quickly put together the information the bank wanted and they lifted the block on Frank's bank account.

The key point here was that Frank had failed to tell them that he had US persons on his share register.

Frank did not appreciate that we were indeed now in a 'brave new world', where essentially every beneficial owner needs to be identified and understood before banking can be done.

In the new global banking environment in which we find ourselves, it is plainly logical that banks want to know who is moving money through their accounts.

The game has changed.

The introduction of the Foreign Account Tax Compliance Act (FATCA) and the Common Reporting Standards (CRS) by The Organisation for Economic Co-operation and Development (OECD) are two significant measures, which impose information gathering and exchange burdens on finance professionals.

More is to come, and part of *The CST Way* is to be ahead of the curve to ensure clients can comply with the evolving nature of information requests from governments and other regulatory bodies.

It goes without saying that we must know our client.

In many cases, the perception among fellow accounting professionals is that there is some perceived 'fixed' line in the sand – that an accountant must seek information in respect of a client and not go beyond it. That is, in our view, incorrect. There is no line in the sand.

In the world of today, knowing our clients, their family situation, their wants, objectives and the things that concern them is de rigueur.

Knowing our client

As noted above, our approach incorporates the following:

- the Fact Finder

- the *R-Factor Question*®

- the *What Can Go Wrong Question?*.

When it comes to assisting clients with opening bank accounts, we also request copies of client passports and other forms of identification.

We understand that banks have to comply with FATCA and the CRS.

The introduction of FATCA and CRS means that for the first time global banks, trust companies and other service providers have to know and be able to show that they know the tax residence and citizenship of their clients. US persons with foreign bank accounts have reporting obligations to the IRS.

Non-US persons from countries that have signed up to the CRS process should be aware that bank account data, in respect of foreign bank accounts outside their home country, will be provided to their home country taxation office.

Banks and other service providers are now under specific legal obligations to collect information from US persons.

In this brave new world, a country can no longer focus only on its own tax law.

It must also play an active role in helping other countries uphold their tax laws and ensure that citizens of those countries cannot use its banking systems to avoid tax in their country of citizenship or residence.

An example of this is in Singapore. From 1 July 2013, it became a predicate offence under anti-money laundering legislation for private banks to allow foreign tax laws to be avoided. Private bankers in

Singapore also have a personal liability for their actions in this regard.

Therefore banks, trust companies and corporate service providers that service our clients will expect us to know our client and help them comply with their onerous obligations.

Many banks and service providers are required to see copies of tax and legal advice in relation to transactions or the establishment of new entities and their business rationale prior to providing banking services.

To paraphrase Winston Churchill: *'Never before in the field of human endeavour has so much had to be collected by so many and provided to so few.'*

As global tax and business advisers, we closely follow where these developments are leading us as an industry.

Given the increasing complexity associated with ensuring clients comply with various banking and disclosure laws, our knowledge of their personal facts and circumstances is essential.

Residency, in particular, is of great importance.

We never accept clients' assertions about where they reside without reviewing their specific facts and circumstances ourselves internally.

There are three key reasons for this:

1. When we lodge or prepare income tax returns for our client, we are supporting our client's view put forward to the relevant revenue office.

2. As specialist tax advisers, many things flow from a client's residency position, and as such it is our duty to understand the position our client is taking here.

3. If a bank requires us to sign a document supporting a client's statement, we need to be very comfortable with their position.

As noted above, the introduction of FATCA and CRS means that many governments have the power to ask for bank account and other information in relation to our clients.

Other international bodies, including the US Bureau for Economic Analysis, can make requests of our clients who are US persons. These information requests often have nothing to do with the IRS or the US Treasury. However, our clients are expected to know that they have to comply.

The list of the government agencies that want our client data is only going to expand in future years, whether they are government or international statutory agencies authorised by governments to collect information.

Doing it *The CST Way*

- Our way is to be ahead of the curve to ensure that clients are ready and able to provide whatever information is requested of them by governments and other regulatory bodies.

- We understand that banks have to comply with FATCA and CRS, and that they need updated client information to be able to do that.

- As global tax and business advisers, we closely follow where these developments are leading our clients.

- We never accept clients' bland assertions about where they reside without reviewing their specific facts and circumstances.

CHAPTER 25

READY
FOR NEXT YEAR

'Mrs Landingham! What's next?' - Josiah Bartlet

I often think about the phrase that Josiah Bartlet from the hit US TV Series, West Wing, routinely calls out to his secretary Dolores Landingham. Aaron Sorkin may not realise this, but those two words, 'What's next?', summarise our professional practice life cycle wonderfully well.

Things never stop.

On or around 14 July for the last 20 years, my good friend, Theo, would send us his tax information.

Scarcely would the tax year have ended before Theo would be the first one in to get his tax compliance underway. Theo was always ready for next year. There was something comforting about that.

We understand that client needs, wants and circumstances are also continuously changing.

As a business, we are always ready for next year.

Always ready for change.

Asking the 'what's next?' question for all our clients is a key mindset we have.

Completing the work for a client for a particular year-end means that a new year commences the next day.

A tax practice has its seasons and its own rhythm.

When the tax compliance, tax planning and accounting work has finished for one year-end, it begins for the next.

As part of the process of getting *'Ready for next year'*, our professional's work through the client objectives as identified in their completed R-Factor Question® document.

Our professionals also note which issues are the ones that should be worked on and in which quarter of the year. Our clients' new priorities come into focus.

Our professionals also review all advice letters for their clients that were written during the year to ensure that any follow-up steps that need to be taken in the following year are covered.

One of the other ways we implement '*Ready for next year*' is through the continual request for feedback to improve our service delivery to our clients.

As part of the preparations for next year, we request all our team members to consider how they can improve their client's position.

The team meets monthly to discuss ideas we receive about changes or enhancements to *The CST Way*.

<u>Updating the Fact Finder</u>

Many clients will have bought and sold assets and liabilities over the previous year, therefore, updating the client Fact Finder is essential.

The process of preparing a new Fact Finder is a great way of ensuring compliance matters are on the radar to be dealt with.

Income levels will have changed and maybe new children have come into the family.

There are lots of reasons to update the Fact Finder from the previous year.

We do this prior to beginning tax work for the client as it is absolutely essential that we are on top of changes to their income and assets.

In cases where client debt levels have increased, this will prompt us to think about arranging a time for an insurance review. The reason for this is that in the event of the client's sickness or illness, we need that client to be able to rely on income protection to service any debts.

Thinking outside the box is what we do.

In other cases, if the client has changed employment during the year, this will be picked up by completing the Fact Finder and getting '*Ready for next year*'.

A change of job will mean we should be on the lookout for a termination payment or the vesting of employee stock entitlements.

Every aspect of our client's financial life falls within our domain to review and think about.

It is not *The CST Way* to say that something does not concern us.

Ours is a personal service business.

In our view, client progress is perpetual and our service obligations never ending.

Doing it *The CST Way*

- As part of the process of getting 'ready for next year', our professional's work through the client objectives as identified in their completed R-Factor Question®.

- Our professionals review all advice letters for their clients issued through the year to ensure that all follow-up items have been addressed.

- Our professionals consider how they can improve their client's position next year.

- The team meets on a monthly basis to discuss new ideas from our professionals about ways to improve our process.

- Thinking outside the box is what we do.

- Every aspect of our client's financial life falls within our domain to review and think about.

EPILOGUE

THE ROAD AHEAD

A journey of a thousand miles must begin with a single step." - Lao Tzu

It was late 2003, when our family returned to Australia after our year-long sabbatical abroad. We had driven over 26,000 miles, seen much of Europe's amazing landscapes and visited too many museums and churches to count. I knew, though, that while the holiday journey had come to an end, the international CST journey was just beginning.

My mind was focused on the international road ahead for CST Tax Advisors. Today, I still feel the pull of the road ahead just as strongly as ever.

While this is the last chapter of *The CST Way*, as a business we have a long journey ahead of us.

We have *just* begun the 1,000-mile journey that started when I founded the business on 1 April 1992.

As days go, April Fool's Day is not a bad day to begin!

It amuses me to think Gmail also began on 1 April (2004).

If CST Tax Advisors can be as ubiquitous as Gmail, that will be some accomplishment!

All our principals know that our journey in Expatland has just begun and we have lots more miles to cover. Expatland beckons and our clients continually call on us to advise them and help them make their lives easier as they live and work around the globe.

Part of the motivation of writing *The CST Way* is to help provide you the reader with a picture of the global firm we have built and what we are about.

We are also looking for like-minded accounting and tax professionals who want to join us on our great journey of 1,000 miles.

Though we have taken the first few steps, we have many more cities to grow in.

We have many more partners to find.

Expatland grows larger day by day. People are moving away from home constantly.

For those accounting professionals that want to come and join us, we believe that working *The CST Way* is a terrific amount of fun. The work is challenging, diverse and very rewarding.

In few other global tax firms are you privileged enough to have clients walk through the door from Australia, the UK or Finland, as happened to me when my friend Hanu Korhonen entered my office in April 1992.

In few other tax firms will you experience the sense of camaraderie and fellowship as you will feel with CST Tax Advisors.

Though our work is demanding, the joy of working with globally-based professionals who think as you do and who want to maintain the highest levels of professionalism is immense.

To my fellow professionals reading this book, there has, of necessity, been a professional practice element to it. If you have found it interesting and have picked up some takeaway points to help you run your own accounting and tax businesses, that is great.

For those of you, however, who are looking to challenge yourself and who want to join us as part of the global CST Tax Advisors team, please reach out to me for a chat.

Please email at john.marcarian@csttax.com and I would be happy to discuss how we can work together.

We will work collaboratively in your Expatland city.

We will attract new expat clients to call upon you as our partners in your Expatland city.

We will bring a new marketing channel and an innovative professional advisory focus to the way you do business.

Being involved with us is something that will bring tremendous value to your existing business and we know that the connectivity you will gain by being part of the CST Tax Advisors family will be very rewarding for you.

I believe it will be well worth you starting a conversation with us.

For those of you reading the book that are not accountants, I hope it has given you greater insight into the business of being global tax advisers and accountants. You now know how we do it *The CST Way*.

If you have made it all the way to the end of the book, then I hope you will agree that our way, *The CST Way*, is pretty special.

You can be confident in the knowledge that if you choose to work with us (whether as a client, related service professional or future employed professional), we will continue doing our best to deliver *The CST Way*.

The journey continues ...